Both Sides of
the Wardrobe

Both Sides
of the
Wardrobe

C.S. Lewis, Theological Imagination,
and Everyday Discipleship

Edited by
Rob Fennell

RESOURCE *Publications* · Eugene, Oregon

BOTH SIDES OF THE WARDROBE
C.S. Lewis, Theological Imagination, and Everyday Discipleship

Resource Publications
An Imprint of Wipf and Stock Publishers
199 W. 8th Ave., Suite 3
Eugene, OR 97401

www.wipfandstock.com

ISBN 13: 978-1-4982-2987-6

Manufactured in the U.S.A.   11/19/2015

"Affection is responsible for nine-tenths of whatever solid and durable happiness there is in our natural lives."

—C.S. LEWIS, *THE FOUR LOVES*

With appreciation and gratitude to my family, my students, and my teachers (especially Colleen, who first read *The Lion, the Witch, and the Wardrobe* to us in her Grade Two class).

Contents

Invitation to the Reader

"Both sides of the wardrobe" refers to the Narnia-side and the England-side of the clothes closet that serves as a magical portal in C.S. Lewis's most famous book, *The Lion, The Witch, and the Wardrobe*. But this phrase is also an invitation to us to reflect on two realities that Lewis held dear: the fantasy world of Narnia (and other lands) and the real world in which we live. In both worlds, the spiritual dynamics of love, faith, hope, redemption, and obedience take their place. In both worlds, Lewis sensed the truth of God's presence and influence that confront and persuade us through both imagination and struggle. Lewis's explorations of a wide and deep range of theological themes, through fiction and non-fiction, were always intended to help his readers grow in maturity as we live out our discipleship.

The contributors of the essays in this book have likewise been convinced that God is up to something, and is calling to us, in both the real world and the fantasy worlds of authors like Lewis. These contributors' shared affinity for and curiosity about the famous Oxford don have converged here to help us see aspects of his work that are often overlooked. From Narnian adventures to Screwtape's letters; through studies of Lewis's collaborators (like J.R.R. Tolkien) and inspirations (like George MacDonald); and by way of reflection on deeper theological themes like human will, joy, and the End of Days, this collection will inspire and provoke contemplation of God's presence in your life and in our world.

Several of the chapters in this collection were first presented at the C.S. Lewis Symposium held at Atlantic School of Theology in November 2013, marking the fiftieth anniversary of Lewis's death. This wonderful event gathered Lewis enthusiasts, the curious, and new fans alike. To these revised symposium papers we have been fortunate enough to add a few more from writers whose interests in Lewis intersected with our own. I am grateful to all the authors for their contributions to this project, and I sincerely appreciate the generosity of Pine Hill Divinity Hall in providing funding to engage two research assistants at Atlantic School of Theology, Rachel Campbell and Matthew Heesing. Their assistance in preparing the manuscript was most valuable.

May this book encourage you and bolster your imagination in your own walk through the wardrobe. I think Lewis would agree that our sojourning inside the world of fantasy is meant, at its best, to help us become more loving and courageous as we return to the real world, a world full of people hungry for hope and love, a world in which God has promised always to accompany us.

Rob Fennell

Contributors

Chris Armstrong is a professor of biblical and theological studies and director of Opus: The Art of Work at Wheaton College in Wheaton, Illinois.

Laurence DeWolfe is Senior Minister at Glenview Presbyterian Church in Toronto, Ontario.

Brenton D.G. Dickieson is a PhD candidate in theology and literature at the University of Chester and adjunct professor at Maritime Christian College, Charlottetown, Prince Edward Island.

David J. Hawkesworth is the pastor of First Elgin Baptist Church in Elgin, New Brunswick.

Sarah Layman is a teacher, historical theologian, and independent scholar in Toronto, Ontario.

David Mark Purdy is a professional librarian and independent scholar from Paradise, Newfoundland.

Allen B. Robertson is an author, historical consultant, and independent scholar in Halifax, Nova Scotia.

Wayne G. Smith is minister of Harrisville United Protestant Church and Steeves Memorial United Church in Moncton, New Brunswick, and a PhD candidate at the University of Pretoria.

Gary Thorne is Chaplain at the University of King's College and adjunct professor in Classics at Dalhousie University, Halifax, Nova Scotia.

Michael Tutton is a professional journalist and broadcaster in Dartmouth, Nova Scotia, and an M.Div. student at Atlantic School of Theology.

Quiet Scenes in
The Chronicles of Narnia

Private and Prayerful Encounters
in C.S. Lewis's Children's Stories

Michael Tutton

A strong plot will drive readers to ask eagerly, "what comes next?"[1] A Christian imagination will ask this of a story too, but is also aware of the psalmist's counsel to break from action to "be still" before God,[2] and of Christ's similar pattern of departing human company to pray to his Father in remote places.[3] C.S. Lewis, in his *Narnia* stories, provides us with some moving examples of this pattern of pausing and taking time. The quiet moments in Lewis's narratives are passages of private dialogue (sometimes interior and unspoken) between the child and a holy lion, which lead to God. They impart a sense of yearning, or what Rowan Williams describes as "an expectant quiet."[4] Three common qualities emerge within them:

1. the *privacy* in the scenes provides the setting for the child to see his or her identity in relation to God;

1. Davies and Wowk, *Canadian Writer's Handbook*, 75.
2. Ps 46:10.
3. Luke 5:16.
4. Williams, *Where God Happens*, 80.

2. the flow of the plot is paused for interaction between the lion, Aslan, and a child, taking on *prayerful* intimacy that includes requests and mystical responses; and

3. the result of this process is that the child, through Aslan, is propelled or elevated into what Lewis calls the *Deeper Magic*.

The Deeper Magic occurs as the Christ-like character assists the child to grow closer to God, a trinitarian process Lewis describes elsewhere in which "we shall love the Father as He does and the Holy Ghost will arise in us."[5]

The approach in this chapter is to search for and detect the qualities of prayerful and private intimacy in three Narnian scenes, and to observe their role in giving rise to the Spirit. The encounters unfold in varying settings: Shasta rides through a rough path where icy winds blow (*The Horse and His Boy*); Eustace is at the top of a mountain in a garden beside a well "with marble steps going down into it"[6] (*The Voyage of the Dawn Treader*); and, in the same book, Lucy's encounter with Aslan occurs in a room filled with books in a magician's island home. In each of these settings and characters we see, in literary form, Lewis's theology of human transformation through holy encounter.

A quiet scene from *The Horse and His Boy*

In chapter 11 of *The Horse and His Boy*, a quiet scene unfolds between Shasta and Aslan. Enveloped by an ominous atmosphere, Shasta proceeds on the wrong path between "more and more trees, dark and dripping," while a cold mist descends and he hears the voice of enemies in pursuit. The voice Shasta hears comes from a creature so quiet he can hardly hear its footfall. The scene is gray due to the mist, and the speaker is not visible. The boy weeps as he considers himself the most unfortunate child in the world. The Lion responds by telling Shasta he has been present in all of his perceived times of misfortune, in his rescues, and in the challenges

5. Lewis, *Complete C.S. Lewis*, 114.
6. Lewis, *The Voyage*, 88.

of the journey, and has played a central role at each stage. Shasta then asks the Lion why he had chased and wounded his travelling companion Aravis.

> "Child," said the voice, "I am telling you your story, not hers. I tell no-one any story but his own."
> "Who are you?" asked Shasta.
> "Myself," said the Voice, very deep and low so that the earth shook: and again, "Myself," loud and clear and gay: and then the third time, "Myself," whispered so softly you could hardly hear it, and yet seemed to come from all around you as if the leaves rustled with it.[7]

In this Shasta-Aslan encounter—with its requests and responses, and this single soul before God—we are witnessing the preconditions of privacy and prayerfulness that Christ himself describes in Matthew 6:6: "whenever you pray, go into your room and shut the door and pray to your Father who is in secret; and your Father who sees in secret will reward you." The word choice in Matthew for "room"—*tamieion*—refers "generally [to] rooms in the interior of a house; the innermost, hidden or secret room."[8] His meeting with Aslan is Shasta's "inner room," where he smells a strange and solid perfume from the Lion's mane and is touched by the beast's tongue. The encounter has trinitarian allusions. Lewis describes Aslan as a source of light, and then gives qualities to the light: "It was from the Lion that the light came. No one ever saw anything more terrible or beautiful."[9] The Christ-image of the vividly alive Aslan evokes the metaphorical language of John 1:4: "in him was life and the life was the light of all people." Yet the qualities of the light also evoke Yahweh imagery, a God "terrible and beautiful." The light-nature emanating from the Lion has aspects of God as maker and creator. Meanwhile, the light that is erupting through Aslan is changing the boy and his actions. Shasta slips from his horse, falls at the Lion's feet, and is without words. Recall that Aslan has already self-identified as a threefold "Myself," with

7. Lewis, *The Horse*, 165.

8. Bauer, Arndt, and Gingrich, *Greek-English Lexicon*, 803.

9. Lewis, *The Horse*, 166.

the third time being soft, and coming from all around, suggesting the Spirit's omnipresence. After his departure, the Lion's footprint is left in the Narnian ground. It fills with water. Soon it is overflowing and clear as glass; it "refreshed him [Shasta] very much."[10]

A quiet scene in *The Voyage of the Dawn Treader*

In *The Voyage of the Dawn Treader,* Eustace Scrubb—a boy who until now has been selfish, greedy, and "a prig"—is turned into a dragon as a result of his fascination with a dragon's lair. He wants to be free of his hideous new skin. Eustace shuts his eyes fearfully as he prepares to remove it. He attempts unsuccessfully to heal himself, tearing off several layers of dragon skin. Yet, when he peers in the pool, he still sees his dragonish reflection. As he later recounts to his cousin, Edmund:

> Then the lion spoke. "You will have to let me undress you." I was afraid of his claws. But I was pretty desperate now . . . The first tear he made was so deep I thought it had gone right down into my heart. And when he was pulling the skin off, it hurt worse than anything I'd felt. The only thing that made me able to bear it was the pleasure of having the stuff peel off.[11]

The Lion then throws Eustace into the water, which stings intensely for a moment, but completes the healing process. The allusions to Aslan as Christ are stronger in this scene than in Shasta's quiet encounter. Eustace is naked and fragile in his rebirth in a pool of water, in what appears to be an analogy to baptism. We also see the Epistles' influence on Lewis, including Hebrews 9:22, and their analogies of Christ's path of self-sacrifice to our own self-dying in order to achieve rebirth. There is also a powerful sense of transcendent power and presence. Eustace doesn't know if he heard Aslan's voice, but says the Lion "told him all the same," in a

---

10. Ibid., 167.
11. Lewis, *The Voyage*, 87–93.

way that went beyond speech.[12] Again, there is a transformation: after the boy acknowledges that the Lion fully "knows" him, there is a final falling away of his false skin.

Lucy's encounter in *The Voyage of the Dawn Treader*

Lucy is a child with a strong relationship to Aslan that has been forged through their previous adventures. She appeared in *The Lion, the Witch and the Wardrobe*, in which she and her sister were present at Aslan's resurrection at the Stone Table. In that novel, she demonstrated understanding of the Lion's nature as being both a "thunderstorm" and a "kitten."[13] When she encounters Aslan in *The Voyage of the Dawn Treader*, he addresses her in a familiar and affectionate way: "Courage dear heart." In this scene, she is trying to find a spell to make the hapless Dufflepuds visible. When tempted instead by a spell that would make her wondrously beautiful, Aslan "growls" and she returns to the task. However, Lucy gives in to the temptation of magically eavesdropping on two friends. Her vanity is hurt by the girl she hears speaking, bringing her to anger, jealousy, and a thirst for vengeance. Finally, she reads a "forgotten story" that is so beautiful she can't quite grasp or remember it.

This quiet scene has the quality of a person with a strong prior relationship with God who prays for forgiveness, gains insight into her own wounded nature, and goes through a process of restoration. Embedded within this, Lewis has referred to some hard-to-recall story ("forgotten") for which we all long. Once again, there seems to be a Pauline element to the quiet encounters, and there are allusions to the coming "glory about to be revealed to us."[14]

12. Ibid., 88.
13. Lewis, *The Lion*, 148–49.
14. Rom 8:18.

A theory of how Lewis came to quiet scenes

How intentional was Lewis's creation of these private and prayerful scenes in the *Narnia* series? Hints of the creative path he followed are found in his reflections on fantasy storytelling, and in his comments on how he trusted Christianity to bring forth imaginative insights.

In his essay "On Stories," Lewis describes his ambivalence towards "excitement" in a plot. He acknowledges the building of tension as a necessity, saying it is natural that when we first read a story, our attention is caught up with the twists and turns of the plot. He also notes that when a story is read a second time, or many times, the reader may discover a lasting and deeper theme in the narrative. Lewis says a plot can become "a net whereby to catch something else." The captured theme is "something other than a process and much more like a state or quality," such as "otherness."[15] Lewis doesn't say in his essay how this quality is arrived at in the *Narnia* series, though it is apparent in the quiet scenes. However, we know he admired the approach of George MacDonald, who wrote, "our imagination is made to mirror truth . . . and when we are true it will mirror nothing but truth."[16] Alan Jacobs has argued that Lewis started writing *The Chronicles of Narnia* to test whether the images that came to his mind would mirror Christian truth. He highlights Lewis's comment that "the moral inherent in them [the stories] will rise from whatever spiritual roots you have succeeded in striking during the whole course of your life."[17] Lewis said that as he wrote, the Christian imagery "pushed itself in of its own accord."[18] In this way, Aslan became the central character in the *Narnia* stories, forcing his way into the middle of both stirring battles and silent encounters. Thus, Lewis's imagination reflects his theology and his understanding of prayer, to which we now turn briefly.

15. Lewis, *Essential C.S. Lewis*, 510.
16. Cited in Hein, *Christian Mythmakers*, 71.
17. Cited in Jacobs, *The Narnian*, 243–44.
18. Cited in ibid., 243.

Prayer: presence, vision, enjoyment of God

Lewis's journey to an understanding of prayer was a difficult process and a joyful discovery. In *Surprised by Joy,* he describes praying desperately to God to heal his dying mother and then, after she died, to miraculously return her to life. Lewis recounts how he could not see God with love, awe, or even fear, but merely as a magician to assist him, "and then go away."[19] It took Lewis several decades to pull off his own dragon's skin and come to see prayer as a state or quality of being with God. In "The Efficacy of Prayer," he noted that prayer was by its nature a request, but added that he no longer had any expectation of receiving an affirmative answer. Rather, the important aspect was the opening of the relationship. The prayer reaches out, God reaches in: "The presence and vision and enjoyment of God is its [prayer's] bread and wine."[20] Similarly, we see how Shasta's questions to Aslan, such as "Who are you?", are not directly answered, except by way of mystical phrases ("Myself . . . myself . . . myself," recalling "I am who I am" of Ex 3:14). Lewis depicts Shasta as content with the mystical answer and the simple enjoyment of the encounter. In the middle years of his own life, Lewis would write in *Mere Christianity* that one of the gifts of the Christian life is resting daily in God, whom he describes as "the other," and thus to lift a burden from one's self amid morning prayers:

> It comes the very moment you wake up each morning. All your wishes and hopes for the day rush at you like wild animals. And the first job each morning consists simply in shoving them all back; in listening to the *other* voice, taking that *other* point of view, letting that *other* larger, stronger, quieter life come flowing in.[21]

Lewis cites the Martha-Mary story (Luke 10:38–42) to highlight the importance of resting in Christ. He advises a busy

---

19. Lewis, *Essential C.S. Lewis,* 27–29.

20. Ibid., 381.

21. Ibid., 158.

female correspondent, "Just you give Mary a little chance as well as Martha."[22]

The longing that remains

Lewis's recurring theme of longing for God, a sensation he calls "joy,"[23] emerges in the quiet scenes of the *Narnia* stories as a result of the encounters with Aslan. As such, this experience of longing starts to be accompanied by the qualities of the Spirit. Lucy's encounter and the story for which she longs, afterward, demonstrate Lewis's view that we are "made for another world."[24] The characters in Narnia tend to follow a pattern in their quest for joy: private meeting, prayerful dialogue, trinitarian encounter, and finally their return to a world where they are empowered to dispense healing, wisdom, and kindness to others, even as their own seeking continues.

This patterned flow leaves one wondering if Lewis was inspired by gospel patterns describing Christ's activities. Consider Christ's life in the early chapters of Luke: his quiet prayer time in chapter 3 leads to baptism by God and revelation of his identity, leading to the account in chapter 4 of his deeper journey into the desert, his resistance of temptation, and the beginning of a healing ministry in chapter 5. There are suggestions the pattern will continue (Luke 5:16), with Luke noting that Christ withdrew to remote places for prayer. As the gospel makes clear, Christ had recurring quiet scenes. They might also be viewed as moments of what Karl Barth termed "revealedness," in that the encounters are a "revealedness of God *for* us."[25] In the same way, the Lion re-

22. Ibid., 539.

23. On this see McGrath, *Intellectual World,* 107–10.

24. Lewis, *Complete C.S. Lewis,* 114.

25. "In the Bible revelation is always a history between God and certain men. Here one man is separated and led out into a foreign country like Abraham. There another is called and anointed to be a prophet, a priest or a king. Here a whole nation is chosen, led, ruled, blessed, disciplined, rejected and adopted again . . . All this revealedness of God attested in Scripture is not just

veals himself to Shasta, Eustace, and Lucy. By this he shows them their own path to the divine. We should also note that Lewis's quiet scenes often have a gospel-oriented quality in that there is human pain involved. Lewis argued that our pain may at times be necessary, pulling us into the trinitarian encounters that can heal.[26] Eustace, in particular, makes the free choice of obedience that leads to salvation in his quiet scene.

Watching for quiet encounters in literature

Looking for quiet scenes means lighting up what often seems dim at first. When reading children's literature, it is revealing to see why and when an author pauses and allows children a private and prayerful encounter with something holy, and how that often reflects the author's Christian faith. For example, Madeleine L'Engle's *A Wind in the Door* creates a silent flow of communication called "kything" between children and angelic creatures that emphasizes the unique identity before God of each child. The children are told, "You are created matter. You are part of the great plan, an indispensable part . . . You have your own unique share in the freedom of creation."[27]

Perhaps amidst modernity's worrying explosion of digital distraction, it is all the more important that children should be offered regular times of quiet encounter with God. Whether it is through the one-line prayer, *Maranatha!* (come Lord!) advocated by the ecumenical Christian Meditation movement founded by Fr. John Main; or the self-emptying quality of the Lord's Prayer; or other Christian pathways to prayer, the process is vital: stop, rest, and encounter God in order to proceed. The quiet scenes in literature are, for child and adult alike, an additional place "where

---

the effect of the Revealer and His revelation . . . It is also the answer to the question: Who reveals Himself?" Barth, *Church Dogmatics*, Part 1, 298.

26. See *Problem of Pain* in *Complete C.S. Lewis*, 603–06.

27. L'Engle, *Wind in the Door*, 186. Cf. Luke 12:7: "Even the hairs of your head are all counted."

God happens."[28] Lewis spoke of the enrichment he felt at the time of writing the *Narnia* series, saying he felt he would "burst" if he didn't tell the stories.[29] Did it help him come more fully to his own way of prayer? He does not say, explicitly. But his work urges us to accept that we will reach moments of confusion similar to those of Lucy, Shasta, and Eustace and that we should be prepared to give ourselves to Christ in quiet response. In this way, we come to know "rest for our souls"[30] as our wearying yet joyful lives unfold.

Bibliography

Barth, Karl. *Church Dogmatics.* Edited by T.F. Torrance. Translated by G.W. Bromiley. Edinburgh: T&T Clark, 1956.

Bauer, Walter, William F. Arndt, and F. Wilbur Gingrich. *A Greek-English Lexicon of the New Testament and Other Early Christian Literature,* 2nd ed. Chicago: University of Chicago, 1979.

Davies, Richard and Jerry Wowk. *Canadian Writer's Handbook.* Toronto, ON: Nelson Education, 2008.

Hein, Rolland. *Christian Mythmakers: C.S. Lewis, Madeleine L'Engle, J.R.R. Tolkien, George MacDonald, G.K. Chesterton, Charles Williams, Dante Alighieri, John Bunyan, Walter Wangerin, Robert Siegel, and Hannah Hurnard.* Chicago: Cornerstone, 2002.

Jacobs, Alan. *The Narnian: The Life and Imagination of C.S. Lewis.* San Francisco: HarperSanFrancisco, 2005.

L'Engle, Madeleine. *A Wind in the Door.* New York: Farrar, Straus and Giroux, 1973.

Lewis, C. S. *The Complete C.S. Lewis Signature Classics.* New York: HarperCollins, 2002.

———. *The Essential C.S. Lewis.* Edited by Lyle W. Dorsett. New York: Collier, 1988.

———. *The Horse and His Boy.* New York: HarperCollins, 1994.

———. *The Lion, the Witch and the Wardrobe.* London: Fontana Lions, 1980.

———. *The Voyage of the Dawn Treader.* New York: Scholastic, 1995.

McGrath, Alister E. *The Intellectual World of C.S. Lewis.* Chichester: Wiley-Blackwell, 2014.

Williams, Rowan. *Where God Happens: Discovering Christ in One Another.* Boston: New Seeds, 2005.

28. Williams, *Where God Happens,* 80.

29. Cited in Jacobs, *The Narnian,* 242.

30. Matt 11:28–30.

A "Short" Theology of Narnia

The Deep and Deeper Magic

David J. Hawkesworth

I n *The Lion, The Witch, and the Wardrobe*, C.S. Lewis offers the wonderful and intriguing pairing of "Deep Magic" and "Deeper Magic." But what does he mean by those terms? For that matter, what is "magic?" For some, Lewis's use of the Deep Magic and the Deeper Magic is simply a kind of allegory, a wink at theological terms; or it is a bifurcated system of natural and moral revelation; or these terms suggest two principles opposed to each other. Yet a careful study of the Deep Magic and the Deeper Magic will show that they are in fact symbiotically connected in the person of God.

First, we should define the term *magic* as Lewis uses it. By *magic*, Lewis does not mean the mere idea of control or the mastering of the natural world, by which one pries open nature's secrets. This form of magic we shall call *weak magic*. In *The Abolition of Man*, Lewis sees weak magic as the alter ego of modern science. We see this, for example, in the ancient art of alchemy and its magical desire to transmute base metals into gold.[1] Lewis also addresses the concept of magic in *Letters to Malcolm*. Here he notes that when he speaks of *magic* he is not thinking of the "paltry and pathetic techniques by which fools attempt and quacks

---

1. Lewis, *C.S. Lewis: Selected Books*, 427–28.

pretend to control nature."[2] Lewis points out that for ages, the wise have sought how to be virtuous so that they might conform themselves to reality, rather than trying to conform reality to ourselves as we have done in the modern age.[3] However, Lewis points out that Nature will not yield her secrets without exacting a price from us as well.[4]

Clearly, for Lewis, the attempt to control Nature to bring about our ends is false. In theological terms, this is part of the cosmic rebellion of our first parents in Eden and is itself a kind of idolatry.[5] We want the world *our* way. As Lewis notes, the selfishness of this *weak magic* lies at the core of Hell.[6] In contrast, according to Lewis, *true magic* is that which objectively brings about a desired result but is not an act of control. *True magic* is also something that cannot be analyzed or reduced any further.[7] In other words, Lewis is describing a miracle, something that is elemental and yet is a profound reordering of the natural trajectory of things. He defines a miracle as "an interference with Nature by supernatural power."[8] We might reword this definition to say that a miracle is a lower law of nature made subject to a higher law and yet, nevertheless, is outside the expected norm. For Lewis, true magic works *with* Nature, while weak magic goes against the grain as a violation of Nature.

Magic, myth, symbol, and archetype

One key reason why Lewis saw true magic in these terms is that magic was always symbolic or archetypal to him. He might well have said that the idea of magic is mythic. For Lewis, myth, symbol,

2. Ibid., 290.

3. Ibid., 427–28.

4. Ibid., 428.

5. Dempster, *Dominion & Dynasty*, 66–67.

6. Lewis, *Complete C.S. Lewis*, 626.

7. Lewis, *C.S. Lewis: Selected Books*, 290.

8. Lewis, *Miracles*, 5.

and archetype were part of the same category: things that were not self-contained but pointed beyond themselves. Magic, such as that which Lucy encounters in the magician's house in *The Voyage of the Dawn Treader*, is something that points beyond itself.[9] For example, Lucy reads that to remove warts, one ought to wash with a silver basin by moonlight.[10] To the medieval mind, which Lewis understood very well, silver and the moon were elementally connected, and like the seas, they were considered ever changing and transitory.[11] These magical elements pointed outside of themselves to higher ideas and forms.

In "Meditations in a Toolshed," Lewis observes that there are two ways to look at things, rather like looking at ray of light. One can look *at* the light, or one can look *along* it. By looking along it, one comes to look at the source of the light: the sun.[12] Lewis notes that the Eucharist is "magic" in the sense that it points outside itself and asks us to look along it.[13] Similarly, the miracles wrapped up in the death and resurrection of a first-century Jew from Nazareth pointed beyond themselves to the reality of the Gospel. In them was a kind of magic that broke the bad enchantments and roused one from slumber, rather like Puddleglum does in his proclamation to the Lady of the Green Kirtle in *The Silver Chair*.[14]

Lewis introduces us to the concept of *deep magic* and *deeper magic* in *The Lion, The Witch and the Wardrobe* when Aslan goads Jadis, the Witch, into describing the Deep Magic. She exclaims:

> You at least know the Magic which the Emperor put into Narnia at the very beginning. You know that every traitor belongs to me as my lawful prey and that for every treachery I have a right to a kill . . . And so . . . that human

---

9. Lewis, *The Voyage*, 151.

10. Ibid., 151.

11. Cooper, s.vv. "Moon," "Silver," "Water" in *An Illustrated Encyclopaedia*.

12. Lewis, "Meditations in a Toolshed," 212–15.

13. Lewis, *C.S. Lewis: Selected Books*, 290–91.

14. Lewis, *C.S. Lewis Essay Collection*, 99; Lewis, *Silver Chair*, 181–82.

creature is mine. His life is forfeit to me. His blood is my property.[15]

When confronted by those who would keep her from Edmund, her "prey," Jadis responds:

> [D]o you really think [Aslan] can rob me of my rights by mere force? He knows the Deep Magic better than that. He knows that unless I have blood as the Law says all Narnia will be overturned and perish in fire and water.[16]

Yet, after Aslan takes Edmund's place, ransoms him, and returns to life, we learn that there is a still deeper magic. This is a magic in which the willing self-sacrifice of an innocent party (innocent because he had never committed any treachery, that is, had never broken the Deep Magic) causes death itself to "work backwards," and the requirements of the Deep Magic are satisfied by his sacrifice.[17]

Magic and law

It might be tempting to see the Deep Magic and the Deeper Magic as two distinct laws, such as those Thomas Aquinas called the natural law (*lex naturalis*) and the moral law of God (*lex moralis*).[18] As a medievalist, Lewis would have been familiar with Thomistic theology and Aquinas's understanding of divine law. The *lex naturalis* is that aspect of natural theology in which God reveals himself in and through creation. Paul speaks of this in Romans:

> For what can be known about God is plain to them, because God has shown it to them. Ever since the creation of the world his eternal power and divine nature, invisible

---

15. Lewis, *The Lion*, 141–42.

16. Ibid., 141–42.

17. Ibid., 163.

18. Thomas Aquinas, *Summa*, Vol. 28 [Q94:1–6], 74–97; Bretzke, s.v. "lex moralis" and "lex naturalis" in *Consecrated Phrases*.

though they are, have been understood and seen through
the things he has made.[19]

The *lex moralis*, by contrast, is the special revelation of God,
epitomized by the Ten Commandments. It is a moral code of
righteousness.[20]

One could argue that the Deep Magic is the *lex moralis*, the
law written on the Stone Table, similar to Mosaic law; and that the
Deeper Magic is the *lex naturalis* that pervades the very air of Narnia. But this is not supported by the text of *The Lion, The Witch,
and the Wardrobe*. The Deep Magic is the law of life and death: it
is the holy standard.[21] But this makes it the unwavering standard,
the *lex talionis*, which requires an eye for an eye. The Deep Magic
must therefore be the law of punishment (*lex poenalis*) because of
who God is: God's own goodness is the highest standard, and God
cannot abide sin.[22] The holy standard is not in itself the sentence
of death, but is the benchmark of what is holy and therefore of
what is right. Any imbalance must be addressed, and in the sphere
of morality this is done through retribution and atonement. In
this sense the Deep Magic is not cruel, but simply blind justice,
itself rooted in the normativity of God's justice. This is why Aslan
frowns disapprovingly when Susan asks him if they can't "work
against" the Deep Magic.[23] Susan unknowingly suggests the use of
weak magic to counteract and violate God's very nature.

The Deeper Magic then, is not the naturalistic revelation of
God, but the law of grace. It has been called the *lex indita non
scripta* (the law placed, not written),[24] brought about by the New
Covenant of Christ. Medieval scholars called this the *lex nova*, the

---

19. Rom 1:19–20, ESV.

20. Pattaro, *Law and the Right*, 49.

21. Lewis, *Mere Christianity*, 3–6.

22. "*Et quidem credimus te esse aliquid quo nihil maius cogitari possit.*"
Anselm, *Proslogion* 2.

23. Lewis, *The Lion*, 142.

24. Bretzke, s.v. "lex nova" in *Consecrated Phrases*.

new law;[25] the New Testament calls it the law of Christ.[26] For simplicity we shall here call it the law of grace.

Remember how Aslan describes the Deeper Magic:

> . . . if [Jadis] could have looked a little further back, into the stillness and the darkness before Time dawned, she would have read there a different incantation. She would have known that when a willing victim who had committed no treachery was killed in a traitor's stead, the Table would crack and Death itself would start working backwards.[27]

Notice that Aslan is not describing natural revelation but the law of grace, the law that lies at the heart of the Gospel. What Lewis constructs here is not a bifurcated system of natural and special revelation, natural law and moral law, but something that was closer to what Aquinas called the *lex aeterna*, the eternal law of God of which the *lex naturalis* and the *lex moralis* are two manifestations.[28] The eternal law of God pre-exists any kind of revelation, because the eternal law is embedded in God's own innate being.[29] The *lex aeterna* is not the same as the written law (*lex divina*), but corresponds more closely to the Platonic forms.

For Plato, forms are the purest reality of what a thing is. Earthly, material things participate in these eternal forms. To the degree that they reflect their respective forms, we can consider the material things to be more and more pure. Lewis loved Plato. In fact he pokes at contemporary educational styles in *The Last Battle* when Professor Kirke laments: "It's all in Plato, all in Plato, bless me, what *do* they teach them in these schools?"[30] The *lex aeterna*, then, is a kind of Platonic form that structures and guarantees all true

25. Green, s.v. "Natural Law" in *Dictionary of Scripture and Ethics*; Bretzke, s.v. "lex nova" in *Consecrated Phrases*.

26. Thomas Aquinas, *Summa*, Vol. 30 [Q106:1], 3–6.

27. Lewis, *The Lion*, 163.

28. Thomas Aquinas, *Summa*, Vol. 28 [Q93:1–6], 51–74; Pattaro, *Law and the Right*, 49; Bretzke, s.v. "lex aeterna" in *Consecrated Phrases*.

29. Thomas Aquinas, *Summa*, Vol. 28 [Q93:1–6], 51–74.

30. Lewis, *Last Battle*, 290.

magic. The Deep Magic and the Deeper Magic both participate in it, to varying degrees, and do not contradict each other.

The Deep Magic and the Deeper Magic are not direct analogies to categories of Christian theology, any more than the character of Aslan is a direct allegory. Lewis remarked that Aslan is the result of a "supposal" in which we might ask, "What might Christ become like if there really were a world like Narnia and He chose to be incarnate and die and rise again in that world as He actually has done in ours?"[31] In a similar way, the Deep Magic and the Deeper Magic are not shorthand for natural revelation and special revelation but are more complex. Natural revelation is woven throughout *both*, as is special revelation of God's moral law. In a very real way they are two sides of the same coin, the coin of the *lex aeterna* that exists in all other worlds, be they Charn (*The Magician's Nephew*) or Narnia (*The Lion, The Witch, and the Wardrobe* and others), or our own world.[32]

Pointing to God's love

The power behind both the Deep Magic and the Deeper Magic is the power to which they point: God's love. Lewis remarks in *Mere Christianity* that there is, in all of us, a common grace from God that gleams through the fragments of the *imago dei* in each person. This shared grace enables us to comprehend right from wrong. This is the *lex naturalis*.[33] The law written on the heart of the sinner still grasps the moral law to some degree, as Lewis showed in the acclaimed appendix to *The Abolition of Man*.[34] Since God is morality itself, it should not surprise us that even in the natural law there is an anticipation of the moral law. The *lex aeterna* is expressed by the moral act of Aslan offering himself in Edmund's

31. Lewis, *Letters*, 283.
32. Lewis, *Magician's Nephew*, 193–95.
33. Lewis, *Complete C.S. Lewis*, 568.
34. Lewis, *C.S. Lewis: Selected Books*, 430–37.

place. Like Edmund, we all need this charity, this love, because, as Lewis pointed out, in ourselves we are quite unlovable.[35]

Percy Bysshe Shelley wrote that "the great secret of morals is love; or a going out of nature, and an identification of ourselves with the beautiful which exists in thought, action, or person, not our own."[36] Morality in this way is a kind of magic, for it points outside of itself to God. This is why, when we encounter Christ's transforming love, we find it "enables [us] to love what is not naturally loveable: lepers, criminals, enemies, morons, the sulky, the superior, and the sneering."[37] Lewis called this *gift-love*,[38] and this is why the incarnation and the atonement of Christ, reflected in Aslan on the Stone Table, are acts of supreme "magic." They draw us beyond ourselves and profoundly reorder of the natural order of things.

Jesus said that there is no greater love than sacrificial love (John 15:13). This is a pillar of New Testament theology. We are told that God *is* love (1 John 4:8,16) and that we love because He first loved us (1 John 4:10b). The greatest expression of love is to love that which is not lovable, which has not earned love's regard. All love must be proven by action, and the most powerful act is that of selfless sacrifice. The sacrifice of Christ is the evidence and full expression of God's love. The power of this act is revealed in the fact that Christ did not stay dead, for the claims of death, Hell, and hatred had no final claim on Him. Christ quelled them all and in so doing, made love to triumph.

The Deep Magic and the Deeper Magic are not polarities. They are not Lewis's attempt to represent the *lex naturalis* and the *lex moralis*. Rather, they are part of the same "magic," which is the *lex aeterna*, God's own self who is love and grace. When we contemplate what Lewis has given to us in these treatments of magic, we see a depth of imagination that is breathtaking and fresh. The

---

35. Lewis, *Four Loves*, 121.

36. Shelley, "A Defense of Poetry."

37. Lewis, *Four Loves*, 116, 120–25.

38. Ibid., 120.

Deep Magic and the Deeper Magic become another way of going "further up and further in" toward the reality of God.

Bibliography

Anselm. *Proslogion.* http://www.logicmuseum.com/authors/anselm/proslogion/anselm-proslogion.htm#c2.

Bretzke, James T. *Consecrated Phrases.* Collegeville, IN: Liturgical Press, 2013.

Cooper, J.C. *An Illustrated Encyclopaedia of Traditional Symbols.* London: Thames and Hudson, 1978.

Dempster, Stephen G. *Dominion and Dynasty: A Biblical Theology of the Hebrew Bible.* Downers Gove, IL: InterVarsity, 2003.

Green, Joel *et al. Dictionary of Scripture and Ethics.* Grand Rapids, MI: Baker Academic, 2011.

Lewis, C.S. *The Complete C.S. Lewis Signature Classics.* New York: HarperCollins, 2002.

———. *C.S. Lewis Essay Collection: Faith, Christianity and the Church.* London: HarperCollins, 2002.

———. *C.S. Lewis: Selected Books.* London: HarperCollins, 2002.

———. *The Four Loves.* London: Fontana Books, 1960.

———. *The Last Battle.* New York: HarperCollins, 1994.

———. *The Letters of C.S. Lewis.* Edited by W.H. Lewis. London: Collins, 1966.

———. *The Lion, the Witch, and the Wardrobe.* New York: HarperCollins, 1994.

———. *The Magician's Nephew.* New York: HarperCollins, 1994.

———. "Meditations in a Toolshed." In *God in the Dock,* 212–15. Grand Rapids, MI: Eerdmans, 1970.

———. *Mere Christianity.* New York: HarperOne, 2009.

———. *Miracles.* New York: HarperOne, 2009.

———. *The Silver Chair.* New York: HarperCollins, 1994.

———. *The Voyage of the Dawn Treader.* New York: HarperCollins, 1994.

Pattaro, Enrico. *The Law and the Right.* In *A Treatise of Legal Philosophy and General Jurisprudence Series,* Vol. 1. Edited by Enrico Pattaro. Dordrecht: Springer, 2005.

Shelley, Percy Bysshe. "A Defense of Poetry." http://www.bartleby.com/27/23.html.

Thomas Aquinas. *Summa Theologica.* Edited by Thomas Gilby. Cambridge: Cambridge University Press, 2006.

------------------ 3 ------------------

Two Paths to Joy

C.S. Lewis and J.R.R. Tolkien
on Joy and Eucatastrophe

——————— *Allen B. Robertson* ———————

C.S. Lewis and J.R.R. Tolkien both wrote of Christian joy to be found in Christ. Lewis's unique autobiographical account, *Surprised by Joy*, recounts his pilgrimage back to the fullness of faith.[1] His final conversion was illumined by that ultimately indescribable divine encounter he called "Joy" – a word with a most particular meaning. J.R.R. Tolkien likewise wrote of that joy, though he wraps it up in his understanding of *eucatastrophe*, that is, the unexpected happy ending or joyous reversal of history. This is a universal, radiant joy that is the vital spark of faith, in contrast to Lewis's personal, occasional episodes or flashes of joy. Nonetheless, these two expressions are akin, related in their source, expressed in the power of imagination, and draw to the center of reality.

Tolkien was emphatic about the two key events in universal joy: the eucatastrophe of history was the Incarnation, and the eucatastrophe for humanity was the Resurrection. This great story, as he eloquently wrote of it, began and ended in joy. Explanation beyond a general familiarity with *The Hobbit* and *The Lord of the Rings* (the latter published in 1955, like *Surprised by Joy*) may be

---

1. Lewis, *Surprised By Joy.*

helpful here.[2] While Lewis is regarded as one of the great twentieth-century lay theologians, both in his extensive literary output and in public radio talks, the depth of Tolkien's theological explorations has not always been fully recognized, though the influence of his Roman Catholic faith on his fantasy writings can hardly be ignored. His insights into faith are couched in the language of poetry and mythology.

Sub-creation and eucatastrophe

Tolkien's insights received their first proper expression in the Andrew Lang Lectures delivered in 1938 at the University of St. Andrew's and entitled "On Fairy-Stories."[3] Tolkien lead his audience along the discovery of the adult world of fairy tales and related literature with their themes of quest, temptation, heroic virtue, and, after one or more grave challenges for the hero or heroes, the fulfillment of the mission, with the so-called "happy ending." This erudite discourse contained two significant ideas (although they were not without precedent in Aristotle, Plato, and Thomas Aquinas):[4] sub-creation and eucatastrophe. Sub-creation encompasses the creative imaginings and subsequent productions of the human mind—art, poetry and other literature, mythology, architecture—with a particular eye toward beauty and truth. We create in imitation of the one Creator, declared Tolkien, just as children imitate a parent. It is an inherent part of our nature: being made in the image of God (*imago dei*), we are impelled to create.[5] God, the ultimate Truth and penultimate source of beauty, has implanted in us that which draws us toward him. In the creation of story, then, be it fairy-story or mythology, there are splinters of light, evidence

2. Tolkien, *The Hobbit* and *The Lord of the Rings*.

3. Tolkien, "On Fairy Stories."

4. See Robertson, "Fantasy Literature" and "Aquinas and Tolkien."

5. He later explored this theme in Tolkien, *Tree and Leaf*. See also Lochhead, "The Tree of Fairy Tale: J.R.R. Tolkien and Fairy Stories" in *Renaissance of Wonder*, 101–06.

of the Light of Life that is God.[6] Here Tolkien was well within the pale of Catholic theological teaching. Sub-creation is of course imitation, and not the whole of truth. Tolkien stated that the greatest story is the Gospel, which is given that designation because it is "true myth." We create, in story, secondary worlds with varying degrees of verisimilitude to the primary world. In contrast, God created the primary world as a living story into which, by way of the Second Person of the Trinity, he inserted himself.

Next, Tolkien introduces a word he coined, *eucatastrophe*, for the unexpected turn, the happy ending, or to phrase it otherwise, divine joy. The happy turn or ending of the fairy-story is posited as the mirror of God's unexpected gift of eucatastrophe in the primary world's story. The Creator entered into creation to reveal the way to himself as the source of truth, beauty, and joy, wrapped up in love. Nearly sixty years after the Lang Lectures, one proponent of narrative theology spoke of the power of story as

> a hermeneutic of memory that is a critical appropriation of the past through the power of imagination. That creative imagination expresses itself in the power of story for, as Ricoeur says, it is only in narrative that we can overcome the aporias of time.[7]

In fairy-story and myth, there is wistfulness or longing to find an elusive realization of a calling to happiness and completeness. This subtheme carries us along the telling of the tales, stirring within us that which we cannot will into existence. Tolkien explains it as the call to God, a flash of blessed vision. Once it is glimpsed, such a longing is engendered that there is no final satisfaction in this life. As Tolkien notes:

> The peculiar quality of the 'joy' in successful Fantasy can thus be explained as a sudden glimpse of the underlying reality or truth . . . [In] the 'eucatastrophe' we see in a brief vision that the answer may be greater – it may be a far-off gleam or echo of evangelium in the real world . . .

6. See Flieger, *Splintered Light*.

7. Cook, *Christology*, 214.

The Christian joy, the Gloria, is of the same kind; but it is pre-eminently (infinitely, if our capacity were not finite) high and joyous. Because the story is supreme; and it is true. Art has been verified. God is the Lord, of angels, and of men—and of elves. Legend and History have met and fused.[8]

Longing and joy

Lewis's personal eucatastrophe was his conversion to Christianity. He discovered that his quest for joy was a path laid out for him – as he believed – by a loving God. His autobiography, *Surprised by Joy*, is our principal source of that pilgrimage and also the inspiration for this chapter. Lewis's personal account of joy recapitulates Tolkien's idea of eucatastrophe by another path.

Lewis's two early encounters with joy were by way of literary revelations: George MacDonald's tales of fairy land, and the idea of Northernness derived from the mythologies of the Nordic countries. These were his passions at specific periods of his adolescence and early college years. Northernness was reignited by reading *Siegfried and the Twilight of the Gods*, which brought back memories of reading, as a child, of the death of Balder: "there arose at once, almost like heartbreak, the memory of Joy itself."[9] Paradoxically, this occurred while Lewis was moving toward having no faith at all. His imagination was piqued, through MacDonald and the Nordic tales, by the idea of other worlds or realities. The joy he experienced was undefined and brief, for he did not know its source other than a release of an unrequited longing. He described its residual effect as "the stab, the pang, the inconsolable longing."[10] He identified this longing for joy with the German word *Sehnsucht*. Terry Lindvall has elaborated on the term.[11] In itself, it is not specifically related to the longing that is Christian joy, but rather

8. Tolkien, "On Fairy Stories," 84.

9. Lewis, *Surprised by Joy* , 62.

10. Ibid., 62.

11. See Lindvall, "Joy and *Sehnsucht*."

describes that sought-after vision or state which can haunt one and disturb one's sense of peace.

Tolkien likewise understood *Sehnsucht* for it corresponded to his own thoughts on the longing and homesickness that a successful fantasy story may engender. This was the flash of the Truth behind our reality: the joy found in God. That longing and desire were deeply felt and their pangs were fleeting. Such elusiveness could never be overcome except by way of a life transformed in death and resurrection. Both Lewis and Tolkien realized that we could not, on our own, create this joy through pleasure or creaturely comforts. Such joy is a gift given to us unexpectedly and without warning, yet it is more real than anything one might materially possess. It is beyond the ordinary and can embrace the contradictory emotions of sorrow and joy. Tolkien, who had personally known the deep grief of war and loss, brought that depth to his sense of eucatastrophe:

> In its fairy-tale—or otherworld—setting, it is a sudden and miraculous grace: never to be counted on to recur. It does not deny the existence of dyscatastrophe, of sorrow and failure: the possibility of these is necessary to the joy of deliverance; it denies . . . universal final defeat and in so far is evangelium, giving a fleeting glimpse of Joy, Joy beyond the walls of the world, poignant as grief.[12].

Lewis was drawn to a fuller understanding of *Sehnsucht* after his conversion, first to theism, and finally to Christianity, through confession in faith in the actual person of Christ. This unlocked the key to joy that, as a gift, offered the encouragement to faith, hope, and inspiration to love that motivates the vivified Christian. Lewis's university fellows and members of the literary group called the Inklings, Tolkien and Hugo Dyson, both Catholics, had played their part in breaking down his prejudices toward truth in mythology and the Gospel stories. Tolkien's particular knowledge and experience in both made him uniquely able to reach the mind and heart of his friend. Humphrey Carpenter, in his study of the Inklings,

12. Tolkien, "On Fairy-Stories," 81.

gave careful attention to Tolkien's apologetics, which blended sub-creation, eucatastrophe, and *Sehnsucht*. Replying to Lewis on one occasion, Tolkien argued (according to Carpenter) that

> Man is not ultimately a liar. He may pervert his thoughts to lies, but he comes from God, and it is from God that he draws his ultimate ideals. Therefore, Tolkien continued, not merely the abstract thoughts of man but also his imaginative inventions must originate with God, and must in consequence reflect something of eternal truth. In making a myth, in practicing 'mythopoeia' and peopling the world with elves and dragons and goblins, a story-teller, or 'sub-creator' as Tolkien liked to call such a person, is actually fulfilling God's purpose and reflecting a splintered fragment of the true light. Pagan myths are therefore never just 'lies': there is always something of the truth in them.[13]

Tolkien, as Carpenter tells it, went on to press Lewis toward the logical conclusion:

> Had he not shown how pagan myths were, in fact, God expressing himself through the minds of poets, and using the images of their 'mythopoeia' to express fragments of his eternal truth? Well then, Christianity . . . is exactly the same thing – with the enormous difference that the poet who invented it was God Himself, and the images He used were real men and actual history.[14]

This reasoning reversed the trend in theological developments, from the Enlightenment to the time of Tolkien and Lewis, in which the Gospels were minimized by the removal of uncomfortable miracles in the face of the new sciences and rational thought, and by downplaying the divinity of Christ to the point of regarding Jesus as a heroic and moral model, or perhaps just another historical personage. Yet as much as some modern theologians and laity tried to dismiss so-called superstition and primitive myth, they could not remove the longing, the sense of needing completeness.

13. Carpenter, *Inklings*, 46.
14. Ibid., 47.

Tolkien did not reject science or philosophy. However, neither did he yield to denial of truths that cannot be weighed or made the subjects of experimentation. He believed in the Word, the eternal Logos; it is words that humanity uses to express the mind's imaginings and visions, reflections of the eternal Word. Tolkien's reflection extended to words used in the building up of stories, words that were linked from sub-creator to Creator.[15] Through this witness, Lewis was drawn back into belief in the story of the Gospel and to life inside the Gospel.

Life after conversion

Lewis's change of heart and mind was made manifest in many ways over the ensuing years. But as a specific link to Tolkien and sub-creation, and the path to joy, one may refer to Lewis's essay on story and fact in the Gospel as discussed by Colin Duriez:

> That is the marriage of heaven and earth, perfect Myth and Perfect Fact: claiming not only our love and obedience, but also our wonder and delight, addressed to the savage, the child, and the poet in each one of us no less than to the moralist, the scholar, and the philosopher. He [Lewis] realized that the claims and stories of Christ demand an imaginative as much as a reasoned response from him.[16]

I have alluded to Lewis's attraction to Norse mythology and the paradox of that attraction during the years in which he had fallen from the faith of childhood. Awakened to acceptance of the Gospel story with Tolkien's and Dyson's help, he mused in *Surprised by Joy* that his interest in the northern European stories was part of the way in which God prepared him for a return to faith in Christ: "I can almost think that I was sent back to the false gods there to acquire some capacity for worship against that day

15. See Duriez, *Tolkien*, 18. Duriez relates the attempts of both Dyson and Tolkien to convert Lewis from his atheism, and Tolkien's argument for the reality of the Gospels.

16. Ibid., 168.

when the true God should recall me to himself."[17] As a Christian, Lewis recognized that his telos was in God, and it was God who gave the ultimate meaning to joyful longing. In a letter to Dom Bede Griffiths in November 1959, he wrote: "All joy . . . emphasizes our pilgrim status; always reminds, beckons, awakens desire. Our best havings are wantings."[18] Corbin Carnell has also wrestled with Lewis and *Sehnsucht* in *Bright Shadows*. He located Lewis's post-conversion understanding of joy or longing within the all-important literary context which again finds resonance with the writings of Tolkien:

> Lewis retained his faith in the basic validity of Romantic literature because he believed it was compatible with a Christian ontology. The sense of nostalgia cannot be valued for itself, at least not for long. Sehnsucht has genuine meaning only in an ontology which has a place for it.[19]

Carnell links Lewis to Augustine of Hippo in the universal scattering of God's truth, which has a very strong Tolkienesque ring to it:

> He [Lewis] insists that longing, conscience, and myth contain divine revelation, yet they do not have the same objective value as the revelation in Christ, though especially for those who have not heard of Christ, they have subjective value.[20]

As Lewis puts it in *Arthurian Torso*, "Every created thing is, in its degree, an image of God, and the ordinate and faithful appreciation of that thing is a clue which, truly followed, will lead back to Him."[21]

Once he applied himself to writing as a convinced Christian, Lewis brought his own insights, scholarly legacy, and study of human nature into play with regard to Christian joy. Inevitably,

17. Lewis, *Surprised by Joy* , 73.
18. Lewis, *Letters of C.S. Lewis,* 289.
19. Carnell, *Bright Shadows,* 158.
20. Ibid., 162.
21. Lewis, *Arthurian Torso,* 116

though, the Inklings friendships allowed for the exchange of ideas, stimulus of creativity, and reformulation of prior beliefs. It comes as no surprise that there is commonality in writings of Lewis and Tolkien with regard to Christian themes. Rather, one may point out that if Lewis was a great expositor of Christ-centered apologetics, then Tolkien must receive his due in like manner. In a letter to his son Christopher, Tolkien expanded on hearing a sermon on the raising of Jairus's daughter and the cure of a boy at Lourdes:

> But at the story of the little boy . . . with its apparent sad ending and then its sudden unhoped-for happy ending, I was deeply moved and had that peculiar emotion we all have—though not often . . . And all of a sudden I realized what it was: the very thing that I have been trying to write about and explain—in that fairy-story essay that I so much wish you had read that I think I shall send it to you. For it I coined the word 'eucatastrophe': the sudden happy turn in a story which pierces you with a joy that brings tears (which I argued it is the highest function of fairy-stories to produce.)[22]

In another letter, Tolkien returned to the attraction of the happy ending motif, basing it in the relationship with humanity as originally intended by God and located in the account of Eden: "certainly there was an Eden on this very unhappy earth. We all long for it, and we are constantly glimpsing it; our whole nature at its best and least corrupted, its gentlest and most humane, is still soaked with the sense of 'exile.'"[23] It is in the restored Eden that Christ offers, as the new Adam, that once more we will "walk with God." That hope enables one to survive the vicissitudes of this life.

The fire of faith

Like Lewis, Tolkien did not hide his faith. He made that plain in "On Fairy-Stories," and described how his faith affected his idea of the unexpected turn or ending:

22. Cited in Pearce, *Tolkien*, 102.
23. Tolkien, *Letters*, 110.

> I am a Christian, and so at least should not be suspected
> of willful irreverence . . . but if by grace what I say has in
> any respect any validity, it is, of course, only one facet of
> a truth incalculably rich: finite only because the capacity
> of Man for whom this was done is finite.[24]

It was this fire of faith that burned within Tolkien and Lewis.
The metaphor of fire is not amiss since Tolkien used it in his mythology of Middle Earth as a way of describing the creation of the
world by the One, or Eru, who placed the flame imperishable at
the heart of Middle Earth. Gandalf, in his battle at the Bridge of
Khazad-dum, declared himself to be a servant of the secret fire,
"wielder of the flame of Anor."[25] The flame, fire, or light are all
interchangeable words for the ultimate Good, that is, God. Here
Tolkien is playing on the implications of *imago dei*: in a sense,
there is something of God's goodness in all created things and all
creatures no matter how slight the vestige now remains. It is certainly being in the image of God that enables one to experience
the secret longing, the hoped-for joy, now realized as the joy of
Christ. The promise of life in all its fullness is announced through
the eucatastrophe of the Resurrection.

Near the conclusion of his autobiography, Lewis remarked on
True Myth and the very reason for joy: "Here and here only in all
time the myth must have become fact; the Word, Flesh; God, Man.
This is not a 'religion,' nor a 'philosophy.' It is the summing up and
actuality of them all."[26] Lewis stated that joy itself was no longer of
the greatest interest to him. It had been so, when he did not quite
know where that gleam of joy came from, but now he saw that not
only does it lead one, but is a signpost, a pointer to what is of greatest importance. Tolkien and Lewis found the path to joy, one by
way of his Catholic faith and the other by the path of conversion.
Both undertook their explorations by way of words and the Word
in literature, and in their own lives were sub-creators. In a poem

---

24. Tolkien, "On Fairy-Stories," 83.

25. Tolkien, *The Lord of the Rings,* 433. See also Tolkien, *Silmarillion,* 20,
and Caldecott, *Secret Fire.*

26. *Surprised by Joy,* 189.

on the life of Methodist missionary William Jessop of Delaware, there are lines referring to the conversion of Jessop and his mother by the preaching of Bishop Asbury – "And they had joy on the road to Damascus!"[27] So it may be said of Lewis and Tolkien: fragments gleaming from the One True Light illumined their work, and they indeed had "joy on the road to Damascus!"

Bibliography

Caldecott, Stratford. *Secret Fire: The Spiritual Vision of J.R.R. Tolkien*. London: Darton, Longman and Todd, 2004.

Carnell, Corbin Scott. *Bright Shadows: Spiritual Longing in C.S. Lewis*. Grand Rapids, MI: Eerdmans, 1974.

Carpenter, Humphrey. *The Inklings: C.S. Lewis, J.R.R. Tolkien, Charles Williams, and Their Friends*. New York: Ballantine, 1978.

Cook, Michael L. *Christology as Narrative Quest*. Collegeville, MN: Liturgical Press, 1997.

Duriez, Colin. *J.R.R. Tolkien: The Making of a Legend*. Oxford: Lion, 2012.

Flieger, Verlyn. *Splintered Light: Logos and Language in Tolkien's World*. Grand Rapids, MI: Eerdmans, 1983.

Lewis, C.S. *Arthurian Torso*. London: Oxford University Press, 1948.

———. *Surprised by Joy: The Shape of My Early Life*. Glasgow: Collins, 1977.

———. *The Letters of C.S. Lewis*. Edited by W.H. Lewis. London: Collins, 1966.

Lindvall, Terry. "Joy and *Sehnsucht*: The Laughter and Longings of C.S. Lewis." *Mars Hill Review* 8 (Summer 1997) 25–38.

Lochhead, Marion. *Renaissance of Wonder: The Fantasy Worlds of J.R.R. Tolkien, C.S. Lewis, George MacDonald, E. Nesbit and Others*. San Francisco: Harper & Row, 1977.

Pearce, Joseph. *Tolkien: Man and Myth: A Literary Life*. London: HarperCollins, 1999.

Robertson, Allen B. "Fantasy Literature as Metaphor for Nature and Grace: Tolkien's Catholic Pilgrimage in *The Lord of the Rings*." Unpublished.

———. "Aquinas and Tolkien: The Thomism of *The Silmarillion* and Related Writings." Unpublished.

———. "William Jessop." Unpublished.

Tolkien, J.R.R. *The Hobbit*. London: HarperCollins, 1997.

———. *The Lord of the Rings*. London: HarperCollins, 1999.

———. "On Fairy-Stories," In *Essays Presented to Charles Williams*, edited by C.S. Lewis, 38–89. Grand Rapids, MI: Eerdmans, 1981.

———. *The Letters of J.R.R. Tolkien*. Edited by Humphrey Carpenter. Boston: Houghton Mifflin, 1981.

27. Robertson, "William Jessop."

————. *The Silmarillion*. Edited by Christopher Tolkien. London: Allen & Unwin, 1977.

————. *Tree and Leaf, including the poem Mythopoeia*. London: Grafton, 1992.

———————— 4 ————————

"Die Before You Die"

St. Paul's Cruciformity in C.S. Lewis's
Narrative Spirituality

———————— *Brenton D.G. Dickieson* ————————

C.S. Lewis's conversion to Christianity marked a profound shift in his personal philosophy. But in what ways did the pattern of his conversion to Christianity imprint upon his understanding of spirituality? In exploring this question we discover a principle that cuts to the heart of his spiritual formation. This chapter will establish what I argue is the center of Lewis's spirituality, namely cruciformity, and demonstrate the consistency of this theme not only in Lewis's nonfiction writings, but as it works through his fiction.

A definition of cruciformity

Recently, Michael J. Gorman has worked through the concept of a "cruciform" or "cross-shaped" pattern to Christian living.[1] According to Gorman, "Paul conceives of identification with and participation in the death of Jesus as the believer's fundamental experience of Christ."[2] In Gorman's understanding of Paul's logic, God, in the man Jesus, is a cross-shaped God, and the believer's life is to be not only shaped by the cross (redemption), but in the

1. Gorman, *Cruciformity*.
2. Ibid., 32.

shape of the cross (praxis). Thus Gorman sketches out a Pauline spirituality of cruciformity.

In this way the idea of cruciformity clarifies the *imitatio Christi*. Being "in Christ," so often repeated in Paul, is not a mystical element in Gorman's reading, but a spatial one, describing the sphere of Christian experience that is "under the influence of Christ's power, especially the power to be conformed to him and his cross."[3] Cruciformity is a better term than imitation because it both narrows the focus on the cross event and moves the focus from the believer to the entire process, including the work of God in forming the believer. Like *imitatio Christi*, though perhaps more narrow in focus, cruciformity captures the "ongoing pattern of living in Christ and of dying with him that produces a Christ-like (cruciform) person."[4] Thus, there is a double entendre in the concept of cruciformity, as it is not just cross-shaped, but also includes the aspect of spiritual *form*ation and con*formity* to Christ. The believer is drawn into the original drama—the "narrative" theology of cruciformity[5] patterned after Gal 2:19-20: "I have been crucified with Christ; and it is no longer I who live, but it is Christ who lives in me. And the life I now live in the flesh I live by faith in the Son of God, who loved me and gave himself for me." Death to self is central to Christian life because it was central to God's redemptive action on the cross. Gal 2:19-20 and its many parallels[6] carve out for the reader what is a cross-shaped life in the Spirit.

Cruciformity in Lewis's Nonfiction

This cruciform idea of self-death is central also to Lewis's spirituality from the moment of his conversion through his teaching on Christian spirituality and his storytelling. After looking briefly at

3. Ibid., 36.

4. Ibid., 48.

5. Ibid., 92.

6. E.g., Matt 10:38; Mark 8:34–35; Luke 9:23–24; Rom 6:11–14; Rom 7:4–6; Rom 8:12–13; Gal 5:24; 1 Pet 2:24; and Rom 12:1–2.

evidence for this claim in his nonfiction work, we will explore the theme as it works itself into his fiction.

Lewis's most popular nonfiction book, by far, was *Mere Christianity* (1952). The fullest expression of cruciformity in his writing, however, occurs in his 1940 theodicy, *The Problem of Pain*, which, with *Mere Christianity* and *Miracles* (1947), forms his so-called apologetics trilogy. Like much of *Mere Christianity*, however, *The Problem of Pain* is spiritual theology as well as apologetic—or, better said, an apology for a certain kind of Christian discipleship. As such, *The Problem of Pain* is a manual for spiritual formation that follows the following six-point logic.

First, the principle of self-surrender, of self-death, is not merely a Christian theological principle or even a human principle. It is a divine principle, beginning in God's relationship with God's self. Lewis argues that Jesus is in full surrender to God.[7] Lewis's focus on human self-death as spiritual discipline begins as a pattern, or rhythm of all reality:

> For in self-giving, if anywhere, we touch a rhythm not only of all creation but of all being. For the Eternal Word also gives Himself in sacrifice; and that not only on Calvary . . . From before the foundation of the world He surrenders begotten Deity back to begetting Deity in obedience[.][8]

Therefore, second, in following the principle at play in all being, "the proper good of a creature is to surrender itself to its Creator—to enact intellectually, volitionally, and emotionally, that relationship which is given in the mere fact of its being a creature."[9] Because it is the pattern of the Divine, it should also be the pattern of the believer. Thus, third, the denial of self is the very act of self-death, yet leads to the *affirmation* of true self: "From

---

7. Lewis, *Problem of Pain*, 32.

8. Ibid., 140.

9. Ibid., 78.

the highest to the lowest, self exists to be abdicated and, by that abdication, becomes the more truly self[.]"[10]

Given that humans can learn to follow this path of self-renunciation, it is important to recognize a fourth step in Lewis's logic of cruciformity. Gorman's emphasis on the *imitatio* in terms of the process as a whole, rather than simply a focus on the imitator, is found also in Lewis. In the way of self-death, it is essential, fourth, that we follow Christ into this fundamentally human activity. It is Christ's self-sacrifice that provides the initiative; our position is only ever one of response. Lewis says, "Our highest activity must be response, not initiative."[11]

Fifth, in Lewis's view, it is not only God who initiates this self-death, but God who fulfills it within us. On this point, we turn to the premise of Lewis's logic of cruciformity: the Fall of humanity. An entire chapter of *The Problem of Pain* and parts of *Mere Christianity* explore the principles of the Fall, preparing for the process we are describing here by retelling the myth of the Fall in evolutionary terms. Lewis argues that paradisal humanity is not the prototype of perfection, but of surrender. In this way Adam, in the natural, joyful self-surrender of his entire whole, pre-enacts the cross. The reciprocal reality of self-surrender was the Garden of Eden paradigm, and it is filled with possibility. The Fall, in Lewis's logic, must have been the first humans' desire "to be on their own, to take care for their own future"[12]—to be self other than Self. This was a lie, against the very principles of nature, and so the entire paradisal melody became discordant. The cyclical pattern broke, and by itself, humanity cannot recover it. Initiated by God on the cross and in the life of the believer, however, God can help believers participate in a practice of death.[13]

Finally, the sixth point of Lewis's logic is that the believer's life changes as a result of self-abdication. While martyrdom is the pattern because it enacts the proper posture of "suicide," Lewis

10. Ibid., 140.
11. Ibid., 39.
12. Ibid., 68.
13. Ibid., 90–91.

warns against the necessity of asceticism, and certainly his lifestyle was far from austere. It would be fair, I suggest, to say that Lewis thought that one does not throw oneself into a Christian lifestyle, but into Christ. So, total martyrdom or austerity—the supreme realisation of self-death—is not the path for everyone even if they are symbolically ideal patterns.[14] Saints, in Lewis's view, would not be distinguished by pristine devotion, social transformation, or the ultimate surrender to physical death, but by the self-death within their hearts.[15]

Such is the logic of cruciformity in *The Problem of Pain*, which then informs his Christian books and essays.[16] For Lewis, both in his own life and in his teaching on discipleship, self-surrender begins in conversion and carries through all of life. It is this understanding of cruciformity, I believe, that explains the tantalizing hints in Lewis's letters to Arthur Greeves in the autumn of 1931, the so-called conversion letters, which contain phrases like, "*death is at the root of the whole matter*."[17] Lewis writes on Sept. 22, 1931, that "The Macdonald conception of death—or, to speak more correctly, St Paul's—is really the answer to Morris."[18] Lewis does not explain here precisely what he means by George MacDonald's concept of death, but the MacDonald epigraph of *The Problem of Pain* may give us a clue: "The Son of God suffered unto the death, not that men might not suffer, but that their sufferings might be like His."[19]

14. Ibid., 91–92.

15. See also, for example, Lewis, "Learning in War Time," 31: "All our merely natural activities will be accepted, if they are offered to God, even the humblest: and all of them, even the noblest, will be sinful if they are not."

16. See, for example, Lewis, *Miracles,* 156; Lewis, "Religion Without Dogma?", 131.

17. Lewis, *Collected Letters,* Vol. 1, 971. Emphasis in original.

18. Ibid., 970. In a postscript to the Oct 1, 1931 letter to Greeves, Lewis confirms this idea: "I have just finished The Epistle to the Romans . . . the essential idea of Death (the Macdonald idea) is there alright." Ibid., 975.

19. MacDonald, "The Consuming Fire" in *Unspoken Sermons,* 17.

Cruciformity in Lewis's Fiction

In demonstrating the principle of cruciformity in Lewis's public Christian thought, we see a particular pattern of spiritual theology emerge. To what extent, though, does Lewis's perspective enter into his fiction? A full survey is not possible here, but an exploration of two of his characters will demonstrate the extent to which "what Lewis thought about everything was secretly present in what he said about anything."[20]

The Voyage of the Dawn Treader (1952)

The *Chronicles of Narnia* have a number of lessons on morality and retell the biblical stories of creation, fall, sacrifice, forgiveness, death, and resurrection in their own way. Indeed, the divine principle of cruciformity is most clearly played out in the person of Aslan in the great sacrifice narrated in *The Lion, The Witch, and The Wardrobe*. Current studies of the Narnian stories abound,[21] so I will draw out just one poignant moment in detail to test Lewis's spirituality of cruciformity.

"Where's that blighter Eustace?" Master Eustace Scrubbs, as we meet him in *The Voyage of the Dawn Treader*, really is a blighter. His family is urban, cool, progressive, distant, and unimaginative. Most of all, Eustace has read none of the right books. So when he lands unexpectedly in Narnia with two of his experienced cousins, he remains a boy in a land where boys can be men. He is priggish, entitled, self-involved, and willing to risk the entire crew of the Dawn Treader to maintain any of those attitudinal delicacies. It is this stance toward Narnia that leads to the events in the chapter entitled "The Adventures of Eustace."

Instead of helping with the work of the ship's crew as it lands ashore, Eustace slips away to take a nap. Eventually, he finds himself in a valley at the precise moment when a dragon has come

20. Owen Barfield, cited in Edwards, *C.S. Lewis*, 10.

21. See Brazier, *C.S. Lewis*, or the scholarly conversation in Ward, *Planet Narnia*.

out of its cave to die—a rare occasion, especially for someone who does not believe in dragons. After watching the creature stiffen and die, Eustace takes refuge from the rain in the dragon's cave and finds himself upon the dragon's hoard. Eustace is thrilled with a duty-free treasure that is now entirely his. Giddy with delight, and tired from the exertion of avoiding work, Eustace falls asleep on the hoard. Then his real adventure begins: "He had turned into a dragon while he was asleep. Sleeping on a dragon's hoard with greedy, dragonish thoughts in his heart, he had become a dragon himself."[22] Having slipped on a bracelet before assuming dragon form, Eustace was in great pain, as well as being somewhat disoriented in his newfound dragonness. When he returns to the ship's crew and awkwardly convinces them that he is indeed Eustace, the change in him is intriguing:

> It was . . . clear to everyone that Eustace's character had been rather improved by becoming a dragon. He was anxious to help. He . . . brought back many carcasses as provisions for the ship. He was a very humane killer too, for he could dispatch a beast with one blow of his tail so that it didn't know (and presumably still doesn't know) it had been killed.[23]

At the beginning of the surprise voyage at the book's outset, Eustace had expected the entire ship to bend its activity to his every whim. Now, as a dragon bigger than the deck of the Dawn Treader itself, he is tormented by the knowledge that his self-inflicted enchantment is inhibiting the crew's voyage.

As the adventure closes, Eustace tells the story of how he stopped being a dragon. The gold bracelet pinching his arm had hurt greatly. One night he saw a great lion coming toward him. The lion beckoned Eustace to follow him, and the dragon-boy was led to a mountaintop garden with a great well at the center. Before Eustace could be healed in the pool, the lion said that he must undress. Eustace tried to shred off his scales and skin, only to find there was dragon skin beneath that layer. Three times he peeled

22. Lewis, *The Voyage*, 73.
23. Ibid., 80.

his skin off like a banana, and three times there was a dragonish shell beneath that layer of scales. It would require the lion's help. He explains the situation to Edmund:

> I was afraid of his claws, I can tell you, but I was pretty nearly desperate now. So I just lay flat down on my back to let him do it. The very first tear he made was so deep that I thought it had gone right into my heart. And when he began pulling the skin off, it hurt worse than anything I've ever felt. The only thing that made me able to bear it was just the pleasure of feeling the stuff peel off. You know—if you've ever picked the scab off a sore place. It hurts like billy-oh but it is such fun to see it coming away.[24]

Edmund assures Eustace that he knows exactly what he means. Eustace's un-dragoning comes at Aslan's will, but Edmund's own metaphorical un-dragoning in *The Lion, The Witch, and The Wardrobe* came at a greater price. He had betrayed friends and Narnia because of his "dragonish" thoughts, and Aslan chose to trade his own life for the forfeited life of the traitor. Edmund understood well the process of becoming aware of one's dragonness and then being un-dragoned by Aslan. As it did for his cousin, Edmund, the undragoning and redressing of Eustace creates a change in him:

> "And by the way, I'd like to apologize. I'm afraid I've been pretty beastly."
> "That's all right," said Edmund. "Between ourselves, you haven't been as bad as I was on my first trip to Narnia. You were only an ass, but I was a traitor."[25]

Nothing in this narrative carries the language of self-death the way we see it in Aslan's self-sacrifice in *The Lion, The Witch, and The Wardrobe*. The language here is applicable, though. We should not imagine that Eustace suddenly becomes a dragon simply because of a dragon spell. He is lying on the hoard, thinking dragonish thoughts, and the enchantment matches the true nature

24. Ibid., 86.
25. Ibid., 87.

of the heart. He was being beastly, so, in the magical synchronicity of Narnia, he became a beast. If we are to believe Edmund, he may have become an ass rather than a dragon; in any case, the cure finds its way through the wound. The play on words is intentional. In Narnia, Eustace became what he was, and it took the Beast of Beasts to make him human again. It took the Lion's shredding of beastly skin to match the actual transformation of his heart.

Eustace's undragoning lacks explicit language of self-death. Yet it does portray well the concept of self-surrender. It is a poignant demonstration of the mortification of the flesh in a children's book. Moreover, as in Lewis's pattern of cruciformity, the change worked on Eustace in his adventure had a permanent effect—not of perfection but in a trajectory away from self and toward others:

> It would be nice, and fairly true, to say that "from that time forth Eustace was a different boy." To be strictly accurate, he began to be a different boy. He had relapses. There were still many days when he could be very tiresome. But most of those I shall not notice. The cure had begun.[26]

The cure continues to work through Eustace, and he becomes a changed boy at home and a hero in *The Silver Chair*. We see, in this brief glimpse into Narnia, the essential logic of cruciformity: a divine pattern of self-surrender whose architect is the divine figure, Aslan; it is expected of all who would be morally good, but by necessity must be initiated by Aslan and aided by Aslan; and, finally, it effects a change in the life of the devotee.

Till We Have Faces (1956)

Throughout his narrative work, Lewis played with maternal characters. "Michael's mother" in *The Great Divorce* (1945) is a disturbing scene that captures a mother in desperate, possessive love—so possessive that it is evidently a kind of self-love, an owning of the beloved that turns the love sour. In *The Great Divorce* we do not know

26. Ibid., 89.

the outcome of the narrative.[27] But this sort of character is picked up again in Lewis's critically-acclaimed novel *Till We Have Faces*.

Till We Have Faces is a complex piece of literature with intentional symbolic layers. It is a first-person retelling of the Greek myth of Cupid and Psyche in two movements. The first movement is cast as a complaint against the gods. Orual, the protagonist, believes she has been cursed and taunted by the gods in numerous ways. She is profoundly ugly, the oldest daughter of an abusive king, and her deepest love has been taken from her. This deepest love is Psyche, her sister, though Orual has raised her as her own daughter and feels maternal affection for her. As beautiful as Orual is ugly, Psyche falls victim to the superstitions of her age and is demanded as a sacrifice. Psyche is set aside to be devoured by the god of the mountain, while Orual falls ill in her grief.

As an intelligent skeptic, Orual is certain that Psyche was not devoured by the god of the mountain, but by wild beasts or the elements. When she awakes from her delirious grief, she is determined to retrieve Psyche's bones and treat them in the royal fashion they deserve. What Orual did not expect to find in the place of the sacrifice was her own daughter-sister Psyche, well fed and happy on the mountain. By Psyche's own account, she really was wed to a god, but the great palace she now calls home is invisible to Orual. Certain her daughter-sister is deluded—either through madness or the evil devices of an imposter—Orual uses manipulation under the guise of love and loyalty to force Psyche to betray her new husband, the god of the mountain. Orual threatens to kill herself, and Psyche relents, agreeing to the betrayal.

Though Orual cannot see it fully at first, her leveraging of Psyche's love actually breaks their love. In asking Psyche to betray her husband's love, Orual is really betraying Psyche's love. Orual cannot understand why Psyche is not grateful for her maternal protection. Psyche rebukes her sister-mother:

> You are indeed teaching me about kinds of love I did not know . . . I am not sure whether I like your kind better than hatred. Oh, Orual—to take my love for you, because

27. Lewis, *Great Divorce*, 97–104.

you know it goes down to my very roots and cannot be
diminished by any other newer love, and then to make
of it a tool, a weapon, a thing of policy and mastery, an
instrument of torture—I begin to think I never knew
you. Whatever comes after, something that was between
us dies here.[28]

Orual resists the "temptation" to bid Psyche be free of her
pledge, and all things break in the moment of Psyche's reluctant
betrayal of the god.[29] Psyche suffers greatly, cursed to wander the
earth in misery. But in Orual's self-involved state, she considers
herself the victim: she has lost her Psyche, and she has "proved for
certain that the gods are and that they hated me."[30] Orual hard-
ens herself to her fate, gaining some wisdom from her experience
and ruling her country with cold efficiency. She holds her anger
against the gods through her life, and upon hearing a legend of her
sister deified, Orual ends Book I, the complaint against the gods,
in defiance.[31]

If Book I is about the filling of Orual's self, Book II is about its
emptying, what she calls, "the gods' surgery."[32] A number of hap-
penstance events bring Orual in her old age to the point of despair.
She finds her way to the mountain of the god and binds herself so
that she may commit suicide. She approaches the edge of her cliff,
where she will throw herself bound into the river. It is the kind of
surrendering that tempts John in *The Pilgrim's Regress*,[33] and as
in Lewis's allegory from three decades earlier, the voice of the god
spoke out of the darkness, commanding Orual not to jump. Like
Paul on the Damascus road, Orual asks, "Lord, who are you?" And,
like Paul, she is not given an answer. Instead, the god repeats the
command, "Do not do it." The god then adds the words that undo
her: "You cannot escape Ungit by going to the deadlands, for she

28. Lewis, *Till We Have Faces*, 165.
29. Ibid., 170–74.
30. Ibid., 175.
31. Ibid., 249–50.
32. Ibid., 254.
33. Lewis, *Pilgrim's Regress*, 169–72.

is there also. Die before you die. There is no chance after."[34] Orual had to die to self before her mortality slipped away on its own or was cast away at her own volition. The rest of the novel is Orual's self-dying, which she begins at once.[35] As it was for Eustace, the resurrection of Orual from her self-death brings a startling change to her sense of self.

Conclusion

Till We Have Faces, then, is a conversion narrative much like Lewis's *The Pilgrim's Regress* or, I would argue, like *The Great Divorce*. Some of these characters weave throughout the narratives, like the possessive mother crying, "Michael is mine!"[36] or as Orual cries, "Psyche is mine!"[37] The organizing principle of cruciformity in these conversions, as hinted at in Lewis's conversion letters and then worked out in his books on spiritual theology, is at play in these narratives. Not all aspects are in all narratives. Aslan's self-sacrifice informs the pattern for all other acts of self-surrender throughout the *Chronicles*, allowing Eustace's story to capture most fully the pattern of cruciformity worked out in *The Problem of Pain*: from divine principle, to human necessity, to the recovery of the true self initiated and aided by Aslan-Christ that works itself out into life change.

In *Till We Have Faces*, the theme of divine identity is one of the complex theological layers. Indeed, the idea of divine self-sacrifice is parodied in the figure of Orual, who pierces her forearm for her sister, Psyche—not in (Christ-like) self-sacrificial love, as she presumed, but in coercion. It is Psyche, in contrast, who lives the principle of divine love and self-giving that Orual can only see once she has committed to self-dying. It is the divine Psyche who initiates the process of Orual's mortification, and Orual follows

34. Lewis, *Till We Have Faces*, 279.

35. Ibid., 281–82.

36. Lewis, *Great Divorce*, 102–03.

37. Lewis, *Till We Have Faces*, 290–92. Contrast the possessiveness of Psyche's King-Father, who will sell Psyche for political stability (ibid., 60–61).

Psyche's pattern of recovered self: "And yet . . . she was the old Psyche still; a thousand times more her very self than she had been before the Offering."[38] Now rumored to be a goddess, Orual sees the deeper significance of the recovery of the divine true self in self-surrender. "Goddess?" Orual scoffs. "I had never seen a real woman before."[39] Psyche's self-surrender to death becomes the quickening of her own true self, and provides the pattern for Orual to follow.

In each of these conversion stories, Lewis demonstrates the principle of cruciformity as the organizing feature of Christian discipleship in much the same way as Gorman understands Paul's spiritual theology. It begins in conversion—a leap in the dark, a dive, a giving up, a surrendering, a self-realization that leads to self-giving—but that death in conversion is only the first dying. All of Christian life is following Christ in self-surrender as God then forms the true self in the believer. Consistently, this theme emerges in Lewis's overtly Christian apologetics books and weaves itself through his fiction. Identifying this pattern allows us then to pursue it in his other writing. I would suggest that the entire logic of *The Great Divorce* is based on the principle of cruciformity, and understanding this principle will help us understand Screwtape's (anti)spiritual theology, Ransom's character development in the Space Trilogy, and the challenge that Narnia is to the characters that enter that world.

Bibliography

Brazier, P.H. *C.S. Lewis: An Annotated Bibliography and Resource*. C.S. Lewis: Revelation and the Christ 4. Eugene, OR: Pickwick, 2012.

Edwards, Bruce L. *C.S. Lewis: An Examined Life*. Westport, CT: Praeger, 2007.

Gorman, Michael J. *Cruciformity: Paul's Narrative Spirituality of the Cross*. Grand Rapids, MI: Eerdmans, 2001.

Lewis, C.S. *The Collected Letters of C.S. Lewis*, Vol. 1: *Family Letters 1905–1931*. Edited by Walter Hooper. London: HarperCollins, 2004.

———. *The Great Divorce: A Dream*. New York: HarperOne, 2001.

38. Ibid., 306.
39. Ibid., 306.

———. "Learning in War Time." In *Fern-seed and Elephants,* edited by Walter Hooper, 26–38. Glasgow: Fontana, 1975.

———. *Miracles: A Preliminary Study.* London: Geoffrey Bles, 1947.

———. *Pilgrim's Regress: An Allegorical Apology for Christianity, Reason, and Romanticism.* New York: Bantam Books, 1981.

———. *The Problem of Pain.* London: Geoffrey Bles, 1940.

———. "Religion Without Dogma?" In *God in the Dock: Essays on Theology and Ethics,* edited by Walter Hooper, 129–46. Grand Rapids, MI: Eerdmans, 1970.

———. *Till We Have Faces.* New York: Harcourt, 1984.

———. *The Voyage of the Dawn Treader.* London: Fontana Lions, 1980.

MacDonald, George. *Unspoken Sermons: Series I, II, and III in One Volume.* Project Gutenberg (2005). http://www.gutenberg.org/ebooks/9057.

Ward, Michael. *Planet Narnia: The Seven Heavens in the Imagination of C.S. Lewis.* Oxford: Oxford University Press, 2010.

—————————— 5 ——————————

"Ticket to heaven"

Lewis's debt to the *Theologia Germanica*
on self-will, death, and heaven

—————————— *Chris Armstrong* ——————————

C.S. Lewis's awareness of his mortality was heightened when he
sat down on 12 Sept 1938 to write to his friend Owen Barfield,
as the storm clouds of war gathered overhead. "My dear Barfield,"
he wrote,

> What awful quantities of this sort of thing seem neces-
> sary to break us in, or, more correctly, to break us off.
> One thinks one has made some progress towards de-
> tachment . . . and begin[s] to realize, and to acquiesce
> in, the rightly precarious hold we have on all our natural
> loves, interests, and comforts: then when they are really
> shaken, at the very first breath of that wind, it turns out
> to have been all a sham, a field-day, blank cartridges.[1]

He continues:

> This is how I was thinking that night, about the war
> danger. I had so often told myself that my friends and
> books and even brains were not given me to keep: that
> I must teach myself at bottom to care for something else
> more . . . and I was horrified to find how *cold* the idea
> of really losing them struck. An awful symptom is that

1. Lewis, "Letter to Owen Barfield, 12 Sept 1938," in *Collected Letters*,
Vol. 2, 231.

part of oneself still regards troubles as 'interruptions' as
if (ludicrous idea) the happy bustle of one[']s personal
interests was our real [task or work], instead of the opposite . . . I did in the end see . . . that since nothing but
these forcible shakings will cure us of our worldliness, we
have at bottom reason to be thankful for them. We *force*
God to surgical treatment: we won't (mentally) diet.[2]

In other words, God forces "troubles" on us because otherwise
we will refuse to abandon our selfish interests—which we need to
do, for our own good. Apart from the impending war, what has
caused these reflections in Lewis? He continues: "I have a lot more
to say on this (I've just read the *Theologia Germanica*) when we
meet. That is, if we meet, for of course our whole joint world may
be blown up before the end of the week."[3] Thus in 1938, Lewis
had just read the *Theologia Germanica,* an anonymous fourteenth-
century German spiritual treatise counseling renunciation of self
as the way to union with God. Martin Luther, deeply influenced
by this work, had published an edition of it in 1518. Recently I
studied Lewis's translated copy of it, reviewing his copious under-
lining, marginal linings, and notes in the endpapers. At the same
time, I began working through his own body of writing, looking
not only for explicit references to the *Theologia,* but also for the-
matic references to the *Theologia's* most characteristic emphasis:
self-renunciation, the abandonment of self. The most striking of
these is a statement Lewis makes in *The Problem of Pain*:

We need not suppose that the necessity for something
analogous to self-conquest will ever be ended, or that
eternal life will not also be eternal dying. It is in this
sense that, as there may be pleasures in hell (God shield
us from them), there may be something not at all unlike
pains in heaven (God grant us soon to taste them).[4]

Here Lewis asserts that self-denial or self-abandonment is
so crucial to the union with God sought by all Christians that we

2. Ibid., 231–32.

3. Ibid., 232.

4. Lewis, *Complete C. S. Lewis,* 643.

must continue to experience a kind of painful self-death in heaven. This is not purgatory he is talking about, but heaven!

Overcoming self-will

It is clear that Lewis got this idea from his reading of the *Theologia*. First, Lewis cites the *Theologia* directly in the *Problem of Pain*, having read it just two years before the latter was published in 1940. Second, compare the passage from the *Problem of Pain* (cited above) to the following quotation Lewis marked in his copy of the *Theologia*:

> Were there no self-will, there would be also no ownership. In heaven there is no ownership; hence there are found content, true peace, and all blessedness. If any one there took upon him to call anything his own, he would straightway be thrust out into hell, and would become an evil spirit. But in hell every one will have self-will, therefore there is all manner of misery and wretchedness. So it is also here on earth. But if there were one in hell who should get quit of his self-will and call nothing his own, he would come out of hell into heaven.[5]

Here, then, is the insistence that we must abrogate earthly desires to reach heavenly ones, and indeed must indeed empty ourselves of our very selves in order to be filled with God.

To see how Lewis absorbs this theme, and how it informs his understanding that we will experience pain in heaven, let's look at that whole passage in *The Problem of Pain,* found within the chapter entitled "Heaven":

> But the eternal distinctness of each soul—the secret which makes of the union between each soul and God a species in itself—will never abrogate the law that forbids ownership in heaven . . . we must remember that the soul is but a hollow which God fills. Its union with God is, almost by definition, a continual self-abandonment—an opening, an unveiling, a surrender, of itself . . . We need

5. *Theologia Germanica,* 205–06.

not suppose that the necessity for something analogous to self-conquest will ever be ended, or that eternal life will not also be eternal dying.[6]

He continues:

> For in self-giving, if anywhere, we touch a rhythm not only of all creation but of all being. For the Eternal Word also gives Himself in sacrifice; and that not only on Calvary. From before the foundation of the world He surrenders begotten Deity back to begetting Deity in obedience.[7]

Lewis then caps this reflection with a quotation from the *Theologia*, as he says, "I think it was truly said 'God loveth not Himself as Himself but as Goodness; and if there were aught better than God, He would love that and not Himself.'"[8]

Reading this statement from the *Theologia* about God loving himself *as goodness*, we may well wonder what on earth this has to do with the theme of obedient self-emptying that Lewis has just been discussing. Bernard McGinn shows us that Pseudo-Dionysius—the spiritual fountainhead for the *Theologia*—says the most important name for God is "Good," and that, further, "goodness" is, by definition, self-giving. Everything in the world is made good, and all the goodness of Creation contains within itself a yearning, an *eros*, for the perfect goodness that is found only in God. But this is not just the yearning of Creation for God; it is also, and in fact it is *first*, the yearning of God for Creation. As McGinn says, Dionysius in the *Divine Names*

> insist[ed] that divine Eros must be ecstatic, or outside itself: "It must be said that the very cause of the universe in the beautiful, good superabundance of [God's] benign yearning for all is carried out of himself in the loving care he has for everything. He is, as it were, beguiled by goodness, by love and by yearning and is enticed away from

---

6. *Complete C. S. Lewis*, 643.

7. Ibid., 643.

8. Ibid., 643. Lewis, in his footnote, cites *Theologia Germanica* xxxii.

his dwelling place and comes to abide with all things, and he does so by virtue of his supernatural and ecstatic capacity to remain, nevertheless, within himself."[9]

When Lewis says, then, that "From before the foundation of the world [God] surrenders begotten Deity back to begetting Deity in obedience," he is making a Dionysian statement. But it is precisely this Dionysian strain in his thought—this insistence that God presents self-abandonment to us as a pattern and indeed a duty—that will throw him into an unresolved tension between affirming a positive role for desire and insisting that we practice self-abandonment. I argue that these (desire and self-abandonment) are not well-integrated in the writings of Dionysius, or at least in the late medieval form of Dionysianism we find in the *Theologia*. Nor are they well-integrated in Lewis.

Nature and the spiritual

Of course, Dionysius shows us, in the passage quoted above, how desire and self-abandonment are perfectly integrated in God (in that God is able to ecstatically go out into the world without "losing himself," because he is perfectly stable in himself). The author of the *Theologia* picks this up, in another passage that Lewis marks, when he describes Christ as being able at all times to keep one eye on "nature" and the other on God. But then he turns and says that we humans cannot do the same: we must "shut the eye of nature"—of our natural desires—if we are to open the spiritual eye that sees God. This, in fact, explains why we must completely deny ourselves—our desires—if we are to come to God and achieve union.

The *Theologia* offers what is really too strict a division between the active life and the contemplative life: contrasting the "secular" life of the body and its needs with the "contemplative" life that reflects on eternity. This is a Platonic, then Neoplatonic, then Christian ascetic insistence that we cannot "serve two masters":

9. McGinn and McGinn, *Early Christian Mystics,* 178. Dionysius was a Christian theologian of the late fifth and early sixth centuries.

we must *get beyond* the things of the world and *abandon* certain material needs of the self if we are to get to God via contemplation (prayer). Although this was a common view in early Christian asceticism, it was not a universal view. One of the prominent church Fathers who wrote against it—and probably the most-read Father in the entire medieval monastic tradition—was Gregory the Great. Gregory taught that the active life can feed, improve, and complete the contemplative life. Lewis felt a kinship for this perspective. He himself perceived the call to Christianity as being something of a call to monasticism, as in the humorous letter he sent to Barfield on the eve of his conversion, saying,

> Terrible things are happening to me. The "Spirit" or "Real I" is showing an alarming tendency to become much more personal and is taking the offensive, and behaving just like God. You'd better come on Monday at the latest or I may have entered a monastery.[10]

Though he never did end up in a monastery, Lewis—as a Christian—still intuitively shared a monastic vision alongside other aspects of medieval faith. He regularly practiced ascetic disciplines such as fasting, meditation, and frequent prayer.

But it is not clear that Lewis ever quite integrated this ascetic awareness with his understanding of the *via positiva*: the ways in which our earthly desires and activities, rather than leading us away from God or closing our "spiritual eye" to him, can, in fact, lead us sacramentally *to* God. Nonetheless, Lewis did react against this harsh dichotomy when he found it in the *Theologia*, as well as when he found it in the twentieth-century thinker Anders Nygren, with his too-categorical insistence that *agape* and *eros* cannot coexist in us, and only *agape* is godly and good. To see Lewis interact with this dichotomy, we turn to his single, terse, marginal annotation on a passage in the *Theologia* that insisted that Christians cannot operate with "both eyes open"—the natural and the spiritual.

---

10. Lewis, "Letter to Owen Barfield, 3(?) Feb. 1930," in *Collected Letters*, Vol.1, 882–83.

Lewis wrote: "In other words we must be essentially *unlike* the Lord?"

Desire for God

Again, it makes sense that Lewis would push back in this way against this disjunctive facet of Neoplatonic mysticism. After all, he very famously taught that our natural desires—our yearning that is triggered by our experiences of what is good and beautiful in the world—can, in fact, lead us toward God. Indeed, calling himself an "empirical theist," he insisted that he himself had come to God in this way. This is the stream in Lewis that is so opposed to the stern Neoplatonic ascetic stream, with the latter's insistence that everything about the natural life leads us away from God and thus we must abrogate our natural, sensing self. This latter self, interacting with the world through not only perception but also desire, leads us (Lewis contended) toward something real and objective beyond our subjectivity: it leads us toward God.

Now, let us see this principle at work concretely in Lewis's biography. Lewis relished what he called the "quiddity" of things. Through walking with his first Oxford friend, A.K. Hamilton Jenkin, Lewis learned to be more receptive to his senses and what they were telling him, and thereby to what is best in the Goodness of things. He kept this attitude until the end of his life. In 1962, in a letter to "the American lady," he mused wryly that his body had now become like an old car, in which "all sorts of apparently different things keep going wrong." "I have a kindly feeling," he continued, "for the old rattle-trap. Through it God showed me that whole side of His beauty which is embodied in colour, sound, smell, and size."[11] In other words, Lewis values his sensory experiences as having led him to a vision of God's own beauty. This certainly sounds like the cataphatic, positive side of the Dionysian vision. To espouse this *via positiva*, a person would certainly need to have

11. Lewis, "Letter to the 'American Lady,' 26 November 1972," in *Letters to an American Lady*, 110–11.

some sense of the value, not only of the beauty in the world, but of the self who perceives this beauty.

This cataphatic understanding takes its most exalted form in Lewis's portrayal, via *That Hideous Strength,* of how a sanctified sexuality can play a role in bringing us to wholeness. In that book's culmination, Lewis shows us Mark Studdock returning to spiritual health and integrity as he joins with Jane in the marital bed, under the joyous superintending of Venus come down from the heavens. This is *eros* in its most potent form, and would certainly seem a vote *for* continuity between nature and grace. Then there is the sermon entitled "Transposition."[12] The burden of the sermon is that *only* our natural experiences can lead us to God, for we have no other mode or vocabulary with which to understand him. Humans, vis-à-vis the Divine, are like "flatlanders"—people living in a wholly two-dimensional world—straining to relate to the three-dimensional world. It is finally only our prosaic experiences in our "flat," merely "natural" world, and the words and concepts we form to describe that world, which lead us upward, breaking through our limitations and showing us—in a dim and imperfect way—that other divine world for which we have yearned all along.

Self-surrender

Perceptiveness about the natural world—keeping that "natural eye" open—was thus for Lewis an essential part of the way to God. And yet, against this positive role for desire stands the contrary thread in Lewis's thinking, which finds self-will to be almost literally hell, and which requires mortification (the emptying of the self) prior to union with God.

His most sustained non-fiction reflection on this theme appears in the chapter on "human pain" in *The Problem of Pain.* It is full of parallels to the *Theologia,* starting with the assertion, "Now the proper good of a creature is to surrender itself to its Creator." By doing this, we imitate God, because

12. Lewis, "Transposition."

God Himself, as Son, from all eternity renders back to
God as Father by filial obedience the being which the
Father by paternal love eternally generates in the Son.
This is the pattern which man was made to imitate—
which Paradisal man did imitate—and wherever the will
conferred by the Creator is thus perfectly offered back
in delighted and delighting obedience by the creature,
there, most undoubtedly, is Heaven, and there the Holy
Ghost proceeds.[13]

In other words, heaven is, at least in this context, a state of
mind achieved through self-surrender. As the *Theologia* puts it, we
have to go through the hell of self-denial before we can reach the
heaven of union:

When a man truly perceiveth and considereth himself,
who and what he is, and findeth himself utterly vile and
wicked, and unworthy of all the comfort and kindness
that he hath ever received . . . [t]his is what is meant by
true repentance for sin. . . . And he who in this present
time entereth into this hell, entereth afterward into the
Kingdom of Heaven.[14]

And again, as Lewis writes in the *Problem of Pain*: "In the
world as we now know it, the problem is how to recover this self-
surrender." But, he says, this is no straightforward matter, for

to render back the will which we have so long claimed
for our own, is in itself, wherever and however it is done,
a grievous pain . . . That this process cannot be without
pain is sufficiently witnessed by the very history of the
word 'Mortification.'[15]

This process of self-surrender, in other words, is a kind of
death, or even, as the *Theologia* puts it, a personal "hell." Lewis argues that the pain of that hell in which we are forced to surrender

13. Lewis, *Complete C. S. Lewis*, 602.
14. *Theologia Germanica*, 35–37.
15. Lewis, *Complete C. S. Lewis*, 602–03.

self is a very *good* pain for us, because its result is to save us from ourselves.

To see the similarities with the *Theologia* at this point in Lewis's argument, let's return once more to that passage in the *Theologia* about hell and heaven as states of mind:

> And when a man is in one of these two states, all is right with him, and he is as safe in hell as in heaven, and so long as a man is on earth, it is possible for him to pass ofttimes from the one into the other; nay even within the space of a day and night, and all without his own doing. But when the man is in neither of these two states he holdeth converse with the creature, and wavereth hither and thither, and knoweth not what manner of man he is. Therefore he shall never forget either of them, but lay up the remembrance of them in his heart.[16]

As its account unfolds, we discover how strict and "anti-nature" the *Theologia*'s Neoplatonism becomes. The requirement of self-abandonment is so absolute that we cannot even safely desire our own spiritual good. The only safe desire is the glory of God for who and what he is. Here is the tell-tale passage, well-marked in Lewis's copy:

> God is very willing to help a man and bring him to that which is best in itself, and is of all things the best for man. But to this end, all self-will must depart, . . . for so long as a man is seeking his own good, he doth not seek what is best for him, and will never find it. For a man's highest good would be and truly is, that he should not seek himself nor his own things, nor be his own end in any respect, either in things spiritual or things natural, but should seek only the praise and glory of God and His holy will.[17]

The conviction of the *Theologia* that we must abandon ourselves to the degree that we cease even to desire our own spiritual good, lines which Lewis so heavily marked and annotated and

16. *Theologia Germanica*, 40–41.

17. Ibid., 121–22.

which he repeated in his own words in the *Problem of Pain,* nonetheless contradicts directly Lewis's insistence that desire leads us to
God. In his sermon "The Weight of Glory,"[18] Lewis suggested that
our problem is not that we desire too much, but that we desire too
little. In fact, he insisted that it is dangerous for Christians to make
the denial or abandonment of self the highest virtue.

Nature and grace

As Paul Fiddes argues,[19] Lewis seems never to have worked out a
consistent understanding of the relationship between nature and
grace: he sits in an uneasy tension between discontinuity and continuity. In taking on a *theosis*-like view of salvation, Lewis plays
with a number of images that suggest radical discontinuity: we are
statues that may come to life. We are tin soldiers that may become
enfleshed, and that resist this enfleshment. We must be changed
from being merely "made" by God to being sons, those who are
"begotten" by God.[20] At other places, however, for example in using the image of a divine dance that we join, Lewis suggests more
continuity between nature and grace. I argue that these rather startling images of discontinuity give us a context for understanding
why Lewis follows the *Theologia,* among other Dionysian writings,
insisting, like them, that in order to reach heaven we must give up
or abandon the self, itself. As he says in the "Beyond Personality"
radio addresses that became part of *Mere Christianity,* "At the beginning I said there were Personalities in God. Well, I'll go further
now. There are no real personalities anywhere else. Until you have
given up your self to Him you will not have a real self."[21] As we
have seen in *The Problem of Pain,* he pushes this discontinuity even
further by suggesting that our necessary self-abandonment simply
never ends, not even in heaven.

18. Lewis, "The Weight of Glory."
19. Fiddes, "On Theology," 89–104.
20. Ibid., 92.
21. Lewis, *Mere Christianity*, 188.

It is hard to see how this can be consistent with his understanding, expressed as an argument in "The Weight of Glory" and as a testimony in *Pilgrim's Regress* and *Surprised by Joy*, that our desires—surely movements of some "self," some "personality" within us—serve to bring us to God through the clues to divine reality we find within nature. How can that be so, when we believe, as the *Theologia* states in a passage Lewis marked out for emphasis, that "the Devil and Nature are one, and where nature is conquered the Devil is also conquered, and . . . where nature is not conquered the Devil is not conquered."[22]

Ruin and rebirth

We find perhaps Lewis's most poignant and direct expression of this negative thread in a late, posthumously published poem entitled "As the Ruin Falls."[23] Here we find a man nearing his end who admits that, though he has written and spoken of love, he has never in his life thought of anyone but himself. Indeed, he reflects that he has *used* all around him—his friends and God included. Only now, as an older man, can he see how this selfishness has locked him in a kind of prison or exile, separating him from his God. But as the ruin of this whole selfish life begins crumbling, painfully, all around him, he finds this pain *precious*—because it heralds a final reunion with his maker.

This image of the ruin falling in the midst of pain echoes a passage in *A Grief Observed*, in which Lewis reflects that his supposed faith in God has been largely self-deception, and that it is only through the painful experience of the death of his wife, Joy, that God has finally blown down the house of cards Lewis had built. As he puts it in *The Problem of Pain*, pain is God's megaphone. Or as the *Theologia* says, in "hell"—that is, our state of mind when our self is being mortified—we are much safer than when we are simply living and enjoying our lives. Beneath the stream of Lewis's

22. *Theologia Germanica*, 175.

23. This poem may be viewed online on a variety of websites.

positive language of desire and joy, we find a sterner creed akin to that of the *Theologia*. Beneath Lewis the joy-seeker, we discover a man who can never be comfortable with his own life as it is, and who must therefore experience a death and a rebirth, and new deaths ever after, even in heaven.

Bibliography

Fiddes, Paul S. "On Theology." In *The Cambridge Companion to C.S. Lewis*, edited by Robert McSwain and Michael Ward, 89–104. Cambridge: Cambridge University Press, 2010.

Lewis, C.S. *The Collected Letters of C.S. Lewis*, Vol. 1: *Family Letters 1905–1931*. Edited by Walter Hooper. London: HarperCollins, 2004.

———. *The Collected Letters of C.S. Lewis*, Vol. 2: *Books, Broadcasts, and War 1931–1949*. Edited by Walter Hooper. London: HarperCollins, 2004.

———. *The Complete C.S. Lewis Signature Classics*. New York: HarperCollins, 2002.

———. *The Essential C.S. Lewis*. Edited by Lyle W. Dorsett. New York: Collier, 1988.

———. *Letters to an American Lady*. Edited by Clyde S. Kilby. Grand Rapids, MI: Eerdmans, 1967.

———. *Mere Christianity*. Glasgow: Collins, 1990.

———. "Transposition." In *Transposition and Other Addresses,* 9–20. London: Geoffrey Bles, 1949.

———. "The Weight of Glory." In *Transposition and Other Addresses,* 21–33. London: Geoffrey Bles, 1949.

McGinn, Bernard and Patricia Ferris McGinn. *Early Christian Mystics: The Divine Vision of the Spiritual Masters*. New York: Crossroad, 2003.

Theologia Germanica. Translated by Susanna Winkworth. London: MacMillan, 1924.

6

Apologist Transposed

C.S. Lewis as Preacher

--- *Laurence DeWolfe* ---

S tuart Babbage offers two accounts of C.S. Lewis as Lay Lecturer
in the Royal Air Force Chaplains' Department. The first account is of Lewis addressing a Sunday morning open-air Church
Parade. Present were junior ranks, Non-Commissioned Officers, a
few Duty Officers. All were required to attend. Lewis stood before
them as apologist:

> He spoke without notes. His voice, which was naturally
> rich and resonant, carried well . . . He spoke without af-
> fectation and without exaggeration, as one would expect
> an educated Englishman to speak . . . He spoke easily and
> fluently, without hesitation, and without gestures . . . The
> majority of the [audience] were impressed, but they were
> not . . . particularly "turned on."[1]

Babbage's second account is of an evening service. Lewis
stood in the chapel aisle as a preacher, facing a congregation of
officers:

> Having invoked the Name of the Father, the Son, and
> the Holy Spirit, he announced his text.[2] . . . He spoke

1. Babbage, "To the Royal Air Force," 72.

2. Lewis's biblical text that night was Matt 16:24: "Then Jesus told his
disciples, 'If any want to become my followers, let them deny themselves and

of what Jesus endured on our behalf: misunderstanding and loneliness and finally betrayal and death. He vividly painted the scene in the judgment hall . . . And then he recalled, with graphic power, the horror of the crucifixion scene. Lewis told us what it had cost him, as an Oxford don, to be a Christian . . . Lewis related . . . hurtful personal memories for the sake of those who were also finding the living of the Christian life difficult . . . [T]his was powerful preaching, born of intense and passionately felt emotion.[3]

In both accounts, the congregations were made up of men from among "The Few," the brave and woefully underequipped RAF of the first years of the Second World War. Many of them would not see the next Sunday's Church Parade or service of Evening Prayer.

Lewis felt duty-bound to preach whenever he was free to accept an invitation. Perry Bramlett writes, "In writing about evangelism and preaching, [Lewis] suggested that an ideal missionary team would consist of two people, one who 'rationally' argues to break down intellectual defenses, and one who preaches and gives an emotional appeal for faith."[4] On his visits to RAF bases, Lewis played both roles.

Accounts of Lewis's preaching without notes suggest he spoke as he wrote, revealing "his rare ability to use exactly the right word in the right place, and of the endless fertility of his imagination."[5] On more formal occasions, when Lewis spoke from a manuscript, "his reading style was so natural and his voice so powerful and resonant" that he held the attention of his audience as he would have in *ex tempore* address or conversation.[6] The length of the few published sermons suggests that he preached for about forty minutes.

---

take up their cross and follow me.'"

3. Ibid., 75.

4. Bramlett, "The Weight of Glory."

5. Babbage, "To the Royal Air Force," 76.

6. Bramlett, "The Weight of Glory."

Lewis's goals as a preacher

Building on my own questions about Lewis the preacher, I want to explore Lewis's pulpit rhetoric, his attitude toward his audience, and his working hermeneutic. What did Lewis hope to accomplish when he preached? A homiletician might turn to Augustine and, standing behind him, Cicero. Lewis might approve. "To teach," said Cicero via Augustine, "is a necessity, to delight is a beauty, to persuade is a triumph."[7] This was the foundation of the first Christian homiletic.

That Lewis always sought to teach is clear. "Delight," for Augustine, was the effective appeal of the sermon, achieved through illustration that evoked the audience's recognition of the speaker's truth. Babbage praises Lewis's ability to choose vocabulary and illustrations appropriate to his varied audiences. Bramlett describes Lewis's infectious delight in preaching.

What of *persuasion*? Lewis the preacher, and Lewis the apologist, sought to persuade his audiences of the truth of the gospel. Lewis the preacher sought to achieve this through an appeal both emotional and intellectual. His emotional appeal was more embodied than we might imagine. Walter Hooper relates an account of Lewis being so convinced of the truth of his message that he had to stop preaching. As it was reported in *The Daily Telegraph* of 2 June 1944 under the heading *Modern Oxford's Newman*, "in the middle of the sermon ["Transposition"] Mr. Lewis, under stress of emotion, stopped, saying 'I'm sorry,' and left the pulpit. Dr. Micklem, the Principal [of Mansfield College], and the chaplain went to his assistance. After a hymn was sung Mr. Lewis returned and finished his sermon . . . on a deeply moving note."[8] Deeply moved and deeply moving, Lewis caught the hearts and minds of his Oxford congregation.

How did Lewis approach his audience? In autumn 1939, he preached to a congregation of scholars. The male students and the younger tutors and dons sat nervously, anticipating the call

7. Augustine, *On Christian Doctrine* IV.12.27.
8. See Hooper's introduction to Lewis, *The Weight of Glory*, 19.

to war. Some were already in uniform. (This sermon was later published under the title "Learning in War-Time.") Lewis began with a question, addressing the anxiety of his audience: "Is not [continuing at Oxford now that war has begun] like fiddling while Rome burns?"[9] He challenged his audience to move with him to a broader view of a world in which there has always been cause for anxiety about the future and never assurance that good work, once begun, could be finished:

> Human life has always been lived on the edge of a preci-
> pice . . . If men had postponed the search for knowledge
> and beauty until they were secure, the search would
> never have begun . . . If you attempted . . . to suspend
> your whole intellectual and aesthetic activity, you would
> only succeed in substituting a worse cultural life for a
> better . . . [I]f you don't read good books you will read
> bad ones. If you don't go on thinking rationally, you will
> think irrationally. If you reject aesthetic satisfactions you
> will fall into sensual satisfactions.[10]

Lewis preached as an insider, whether at Oxford or among RAF officers. He identified with congregations made up of educated, affluent lay men and women. His peers would appreciate his concern, understand his vocabulary, be familiar with his literary and historical references, and laugh with him when he identified absurdities. Lewis devoted the last, brief movement of the sermon to "enemies which war raises up against the scholar": excitement, "the tendency to think and feel about the war when we had intended to think about our work," and frustration, "the feeling that we shall not have time to finish."

When he named the third enemy, fear, Lewis came as close as he ever did to violating the homiletical transaction. The insider preacher can be trusted to speak indirectly of matters of real concern. In the last moments of the sermon Lewis named the greatest fear present in his audience: "War threatens us with death and pain." Even on the page, a shift in voice is clear.

9. Lewis, "Learning in War-Time," 45.
10. Ibid., 46–48.

But there is no question of death or life for any of us; only a question of this death or that—a machine gun bullet now or a cancer forty years later. What does war do to death? It certainly does not make it more frequent: 100 percent of us die, and the percentage cannot be increased. [War] puts several deaths earlier[.][11]

Lewis named this fear, but then rushed to place it in a broader context, as he did in his treatment of anxiety earlier in the sermon. He even claimed death in battle was instantaneous, and less to be feared than a lingering death due to illness. War called all who entered it to prepare for death, but Christians should always be ready to die. In his concluding words, Lewis reiterated his call to scholarship as duty. He saw his congregation as fellow disciples, bound to be faithful to their duty to God.

Lewis's hermeneutic

What can the homiletician say of Lewis's working hermeneutic? Lewis had no doubts about the Bible's divine origin. He held that the Bible was to be believed because the church had always believed it. He accused scholars of undermining the faith of "uneducated" laity, among whom Lewis counted himself. In "Fern-seed and Elephants," he warned theological students at Westcott House, Cambridge, against the teaching of modern Biblical and theological scholars like Albert Schweitzer, Rudolf Bultmann, Paul Tillich, and Alec Vidler. Lewis said such critics lacked real knowledge of critical method. "They seem to me to lack literary judgment, to be imperceptive about the very quality of the texts they are reading." He imagined a scholar, so immersed in his study of New Testament texts and commentaries that he "lacks any standard of comparison such as can only grow from a wide and deep and genial experience of literature in general."[12] This lack made Lewis a critic of the critics:

11. Ibid., 52–53.
12. Lewis, "Fern-seed," 106–07.

Dr. Bultmann never wrote a gospel. Has the experience of his learned, specialized, and no doubt meritorious, life really given him any power of seeing into the minds of those long dead men who were caught up into what, on any view, must be regarded as the central religious experience of the whole human race?[13]

Those who lacked the expertise to read critically lower forms of literature were hardly qualified to pass judgment on the highest form of literature. Lewis, however, was overflowing with literary experience and judgment, if not with formal theological education. He approached holy writ with appropriate reverence and scholarship.

A homiletician might be tempted to read Paul Ricoeur back into C.S. Lewis and describe the latter's approach to Scripture as "informed first naiveté." It was informed by a mixture of faith and reverently applied literary criticism, not by critical awareness born of textual study. Lewis was not a literalist. He recognized, by his own informed judgment, literary types among texts. He defended historicity while pointing to the mythic, symbolic power of Biblical narrative.

In *The Allegory of Love*, we find the genesis of his biblical hermeneutic, supported by a quote from seventeenth-century polymath Thomas Browne:

The attempt to read . . . something else through its sensible imitations, to see the archetype in the copy, is what I mean by symbolism or sacramentalism. It is, in fine, "the philosophy of Hermes that this visible world is but a picture of the invisible, wherein, as a portrait, things are not truly but in equivocal shapes, as they counterfeit some real substance in that visible fabric[.]"

He went on to distinguish between the work of the allegorist and the symbolist:

The allegorist leaves the given—his own passions—to talk of that which is confessedly less real, which is a

13. Ibid.,118.

fiction. The symbolist leaves the given to find that which is more real. To put the difference in another way, for the symbolist it is we who are the allegory . . . the world which we mistake for reality is the flat outline of that which elsewhere veritably is in all the round of its un-imaginable dimensions.[14]

When he opened the Bible and took up the work of Hermes, Lewis thus applied his own brand of neoplatonism, which he called "transposition".

Transposition

In the sermon entitled "Transposition," Lewis poured heart and soul into a demonstration and defense of his hermeneutic. He preached the sermon on Whitsunday, May 28, 1944, in Mansfield College Chapel, Oxford. It was later published with some amendments in English and Italian. The text was the Pentecost story from the second chapter of Acts and, specifically, the manifestation of the Holy Spirit's power that enabled the first Christians to "speak in other languages."[15] Lewis also referred to Paul's "embarrassed" treatment of speaking with tongues in 1 Corinthians 12–14. Paul's reference to his own experience of tongues in 1 Corinthians 14:18 gave Lewis pretext for his treatment of the Pentecost phenomenon. If Paul experienced it, even if he didn't think it important, it must be real.

Lewis had at least heard of revivalist meetings where participants "burst out into a torrent of what appears to be gibberish." He confessed, "*glossolalia* has often been a stumbling-block to me. It is, to be frank, an embarrassing phenomenon."[16] He said that most instances of babbling were signs of hysteria. Yet the Holy Spirit gave this gift to fulfill what Jesus had predicted before he ascended to Heaven:

14. Lewis, *Allegory of Love*, 45.

15. Acts 2:4.

16. Lewis, "Transposition," 9.

It looks, therefore, as if we shall have to say that the very same phenomenon which is sometimes not only natural but even pathological is at other times (or at least at one other time) the organ of the Holy Ghost.[17]

Glossolalia, then, could be both a sign of communion in the Holy Spirit *and* an indication of insanity.

Lewis urged his congregation to think, if only briefly, of love and lust: "they usually end in what is, physically, the same act." Likewise, vengeance and justice. Emotional life was higher than sensation; not morally higher, "but richer, more varied, more subtle." Lewis assumed most human beings knew this. But the correspondence between higher and lower was not one for one: "The transposition of the richer into the poorer must, so to speak, be algebraical, not arithmetical." One example was the writing of "a language with twenty-two vowel sounds in an alphabet with only five vowel characters," which would require one to "give each of those five characters more than one value."[18]

Without using the word, Lewis spoke of the sacramental. But he declared transposition was not always symbolism. Such was the power of the higher reality that it could draw the lower into itself:

The sensation which accompanies joy becomes itself joy; we can hardly choose but say 'incarnates joy'. If this is so, then I venture to suggest, though with great doubt and in the most provisional way, that the concept of Transposition may have some contribution to make to the theology—or at least to the philosophy—of the Incarnation.[19]

In "Transposition," Lewis employed a common homiletical technique. He teased a problem out of a text or topic and went on to offer a solution. As an insider, he assumed his audience would recognize the problem and be willing to pursue an answer along with him. Lewis concluded the sermon by naming a greater problem and reframing the original question. He wasn't just addressing

17. Ibid., 10.
18. Ibid., 12–13.
19. Ibid., 19.

his own and his audience's discomfort with religious ecstasy. He offered transposition as a way to live with the many manifestations of the inevitable tension between "Spirit and Nature, God and Man."

Lewis preached in a time when major newspapers paid close attention to what was said from prominent pulpits, and educated men and women sat beneath those pulpits with high expectations. "Oxford's modern Newman" was, by his own estimation, Jack Lewis, uneducated layman. Those who heard him preach may not have thought of him as a new Newman, but they were unlikely to have thought him an unsophisticated, amateur theologian.

Lewis maintained a distinction between apologetic and homiletic, but his sermons were no less arguments for the good sense of Christian belief than his better-known essays and published addresses. In his sermons, he sought to persuade his intellectual and social peers, who were also fellow-disciples, of the enduring value of the faith he believed they would be called on to defend.

Bibliography

Augustine, *On Christian Doctrine*. Christian Classics Ethereal Library. http://www.ccel.org/ccel/augustine/doctrine.i.html.

Babbage, Stuart Barton. "To the Royal Air Force." In *C.S. Lewis: Speaker and Teacher*, edited by Carolyn Keefe, 85–102. Grand Rapids, MI: Zondervan, 1971.

Bramlett, Perry. "The Weight of Glory: C.S. Lewis as Preacher." http://www.preaching.com/resources/past-masters/11563667/.

Lewis, C.S. *The Allegory of Love: A Study in Medieval Tradition*. New York: Oxford University Press, 1958.

———. "Fern-seed and Elephants." In *Fern-seed and Elephants and Other Essays on Christianity*, edited by Walter Hooper, 104–25. Glasgow: Collins, 1975.

———. "Learning in War-Time." In *Transposition and Other Addresses*, 45–54. London: Geoffrey Bles, 1949.

———. "Transposition." In *Transposition and Other Addresses*, 9–20. London: Geoffrey Bles, 1949.

———. *The Weight of Glory and Other Addresses*. New York: Simon and Schuster, 1980.

7

Baptized but not Sanctified

George MacDonald and the Fantastic Baptism
of the Imagination of C.S. Lewis

——————— *Gary Thorne* ———————

M any of my friends consider C.S. Lewis to be their Virgil, sent
to guide them to the very edge of the Paradiso, as Virgil did
for Dante in *The Divine Comedy*. But Lewis never played that role
for me. In the late 1970s I read the *Narnia* series and was led no-
where, mainly because of the influence of Dr. Terrance Prendergast
SJ (now Archbishop of Ottawa), who had convinced me to honor
parable and to despise allegory. I could see in Lewis nothing but
allegory: didactic truth of the Christian religion dressed up in a
charming Narnia. Every detail was meant to point to something
else. These were children's books for children, "where lampposts
come to life and grow like trees; in which animals, but not all
animals, talk; . . . in which trees are personalities that walk and
sing[;]" and in which there are many memorable figures such as
Aslan, Reepicheep, Puddleglum, and more.[1] Narnia is the "magical
world that Digory Kirke and Polly Plummer first discover" and
that others will also visit.[2]

In my first reading of the *Narnia* books, the allegory was clev-
er but hardly insightful. Since that time, I've discovered that others,

1. Johnston, "Image and Content," 254.
2. Ibid., 254.

most famously J.R.R. Tolkien, disliked the *Narnia* stories for the same reason. As Dwight Longenecker notes, "Tolkien disliked allegory, and the Narnia tales were too allegorical for his taste. Lewis protested that they were not allegory . . . but an analogy. While it is true that the characters in Narnia do not have a one on one allegorical relationship with abstract truths, they do point clearly to greater truths and greater characters in the Christian story."[3] This kind of didacticism is what Tolkien rejected. Tolkien's assessment of Lewis precisely described my own initial reaction to Narnia.

About fifteen years after I had entered the wardrobe and determined that I would not return for further adventures, I discovered the fairy tales of George MacDonald and was hooked. These were something entirely different and insightful. At the time I did not know of any relation between MacDonald and Lewis, let alone the decisive influence that MacDonald had on Lewis. When I read how Lewis describes his imagination as having been "baptized" by the reading of George MacDonald, I became very curious.

Once the influence of MacDonald was pointed out, I could see the obvious borrowings. MacDonald's *Lilith,* for instance, seems to have influenced Lewis's *Till We Have Faces* and *The Last Battle*; likewise, I could see the animal characters in MacDonald's *The Princess and Curdie* reflected in Lewis's creatures in the *Narnia*.[4] Apart from these obvious parallels, I still considered their literary forms to be very different.

MacDonald's influence on Lewis

Thus I ask two questions in this chapter. First, what did Lewis mean when he said that his imagination had been baptized by MacDonald? Second, why do I remain so unconvinced? Or, as my title suggests, if indeed Lewis's imagination was baptized by MacDonald, it certainly was not "sanctified." Lewis's imagination did not grow and develop in the genre of MacDonald's fairy tales.

3. Longenecker, "Tolkien's 'No' to Narnia."

4. Seper, "C.S. Lewis."

Initially, then, I'll let Lewis speak in his own words of his debt to MacDonald. Next, I'll briefly consider MacDonald's *Phantastes*. My best hope is that you know Lewis much better than I do, and will bridge the gap ahead of me to see how indeed MacDonald and Lewis are not at cross purposes.

In his preface to *George MacDonald, An Anthology*, Lewis speaks extensively of his debt to MacDonald:

> Most myths were made in prehistoric times, and, I suppose, not consciously made by individuals at all. But every now and then there occurs in the modern world a genius—a Kafka or a Novalis—who can make such a story. MacDonald is the greatest genius of this kind whom I know . . . I know hardly any other writer who seems to be closer, or more continually close, to the Spirit of Christ Himself.

Lewis goes so far as to call MacDonald his *master*: "indeed I fancy I have never written a book in which I did not quote from him . . . Honesty drives me to emphasize it." He continues:

> What it [MacDonald's *Phantastes*] actually did to me was to convert, even to baptize . . . my imagination. It did nothing to my intellect nor (at that time) to my conscience. Their turn came far later and with the help of many other books and men. But when the process was complete . . . I found that I was still with MacDonald and that he had accompanied me all the way and that I was now at last ready to hear from him much that he could not have told me at that first meeting. But in a sense, what he was now telling me was the very same that he had told me from the beginning.

Thus Lewis describes MacDonald's influence on him. In the final sentence of his testimony, he articulates precisely the genius of MacDonald: "The quality which had enchanted me in his imaginative works turned out to be the quality of the real universe, the divine, magical, terrifying, and ecstatic reality in which we all live."[5]

5. These excerpts are taken from the preface to Lewis, *George MacDonald*.

There is one other place that Lewis speaks of MacDonald's impact on him. In *Surprised by Joy*, he remarks on coming upon *Phantastes* at the culmination of his search for joy. Remember that for Lewis, at this stage of his journey, "joy was like a small glimpse at the end of a rainbow, intriguing him to further seek out its source."[6] In reading *Phantastes*, he found joy's fulfillment. He now realized that "this object of desire could be obtained in *this* waking real world in which he had lived all along."[7]

> For I now perceived that while the air of the new region made all my erotic and magical perversions of Joy look like sordid trumpery, it had no such disenchanting power over the bread upon the table or the coals in the grate. That was the marvel. Up till now each visitation of Joy had left the common world momentarily a desert . . . Even when real clouds or trees had been the material of the vision, they had been so only by reminding me of another world; and I did not like the return to ours. But now I saw the bright shadow coming out of the book into the real world and resting there, transforming all common things and yet itself unchanged.[8]

Here, again, Lewis describes MacDonald's fairy tales in language akin to a theophany, that is, a sacramental vision of the created order. In describing the world as theophany, the notion of the supernatural is not about anything other than the ordinary. The ordinary remains in its integrity, but the spiritual reality shines through.

Too didactic, too dogmatic

As Lewis read him, MacDonald allows us to see the world with new eyes: to live in it, be present to it, and to love it for what it is. But I think that this is precisely what Lewis himself does not accomplish. Rather than describing the natural world as revealing the supernatural, and the supernatural as revealing the true character

6. Seper, "C.S. Lewis."
7. Ibid.
8. Lewis, *Surprised by Joy*, 181.

of the natural, Lewis rather gives a didactic and doctrinal commentary on this world. Lewis describes our world in Narnia, but adds nothing new to it. He never gets away from the didactic and the dogmatic. This is what bothered J.R.R. Tolkien: what might be described as Lewis's Protestantism. That is, on the one hand evangelical folk like N.T. Wright become impatient with Lewis because they judge Lewis's notion of Christ to be too Platonic and Neoplatonic[9] and thus not grounded sufficiently in the Scriptures, specifically in Hebrew culture and thought. On the other hand, folk like Tolkien are critical of Lewis because he refuses to allow the fairy tale to work out redemption on its own terms. For example, Lewis talks about beginning the *Narnia* series with an image he had had for a long time. He says, "The *Lion* all began with a picture of a Faun carrying an umbrella and parcels in a snowy wood. This picture had been in my mind since I was about sixteen. Then one day, when I was about forty, I said to myself: 'Let's try to make a story about it.'"[10] And so Lewis began to construct his Narnia. He had the entire first draft completed without even a thought for an Aslan. It was only later that he thought about how the Savior, Jesus, might appear in Narnia. Clearly, thought Lewis, it would be as a talking animal. Thus Aslan, a lion and a Biblical image (think of the Lion of Judah in Rev. 5:5), was added to Narnia. In *The Voyage of the Dawn Treader*, Aslan tells the children that the Aslan whom they experienced in Narnia will help them understand another Aslan of a different name in their world.

George MacDonald would not have introduced or inserted any such Aslan in a fairy tale. The idea of an Aslan would have had to grow out of the laws of the myth itself. As MacDonald says in his 1893 article "The Fantastic Imagination,"

> His world once invented, the highest law that comes next
> into play is, that there shall be harmony between the laws
> by which the new world has begun to exist; and in the
> process of his creation, the inventor must hold by those

9. Lewis was influenced by Charles Williams's *Place of the Lion*, a fantasy that precisely invokes the Platonic Forms.

10. Lewis, "It All Began with a Picture," 42.

laws . . . to live a moment in an imagined world, we must see the laws of its existence obeyed.

MacDonald goes on to comment on allegory and his impatience with it:

> A fairytale is not an allegory. There may be allegory in it, but it is not an allegory. He must be an artist indeed who can, in any mode, produce a strict allegory that is not a weariness to the spirit.[11]

Phantastes

Finally, what did Lewis see in *Phantastes*, written at the beginning of MacDonald's career? It offers a beautiful affirmation of the inherent goodness of all things—the entire cosmos, every element of the created order—and identifies the source of evil as the will of the self. In this novel, we find "the story of a young man who unknowingly 'set out to find [his] Ideal.'"[12] Here MacDonald inserts Platonic idealism: "the conception of physical things as images of transcendent ideals which a person should seek to understand."[13] The transcendent and ideal are embodied in the particular, and the spiritual in the natural. As Salvey notes,

> Mirroring the experience in Plato's 'Allegory of the Cave' from *The Republic*, Anodos [the lead character of *Phantastes*] is completely unaware of the existence of the ideal, the goal of life, when he enters fairyland, an ignorance betrayed in his constant bewilderment and aimless wandering. However, when he sees the lady imprisoned in the marble, the existence of the ideal flashes upon him.[14]

Anodos's insight into the shadow and the true Form illustrates MacDonald's "Augustinian conception of evil and the self."[15]

11. MacDonald, "The Fantastic Imagination."
12. Salvey, "Riddled With Evil," 19.
13. Ibid., 19.
14. Ibid., 19.
15. Ibid., 22.

Despite his perverse impulses and disordered desire, Anodos in time grows in holiness and at last looks outside himself.

For Lewis and MacDonald both, a fairy tale is held together by the spiritual and moral laws of the cosmos. Indeed, there is a sense that in the fairy tale, the moral order encompasses the whole of the created order. Indeed, the natural laws reflect the moral law and the moral struggle. Truth, says MacDonald, is a Person, not dogma. The whole of the created order is thus personal: creation inheres within Christ. The fairy tale allows a contemplative stance toward landscape and nature that both respects its particularity and integrity, yet allows the universal (Beauty, Goodness, Truth) to be present in and through it.

What Lewis so admires in MacDonald, he himself does not achieve. In Lewis's work, the fairy tale is always pressed into service and becomes allegory. MacDonald allows it to remain fairy tale. Thus I suggest that while Lewis's imagination may have been baptized by his reading of George MacDonald, it was, unfortunately, never sanctified: it failed to actualize the imaginative rebirth he so admired in his literary mentor.

Bibliography

Johnston, Robert K. "Image and Content: The Tension in C.S. Lewis' *Chronicles of Narnia*." *Journal of the Evangelical Theological Society* 20 (Summer 1977) 253–64.

Lewis, C.S., ed. *George MacDonald: An Anthology*. New York: MacMillan, 1978.

————. "It All Began with a Picture." In *Of Other Worlds: Essays and Stories,* edited by Walter Hooper, 42. London: Geoffrey Bles, 1966.

————. *Surprised by Joy.* Orlando, FL: Harcourt, 1984.

Longenecker, Dwight. "Tolkien's 'No' to Narnia." http://www.patheos.com/blogs/standingonmyhead/tolkiens-no-to-narnia

MacDonald, George. "The Fantastic Imagination." http://gaslight.mtroyal.ca/ortsx14.htm.

Salvey, Courtney. "Riddled with Evil: Fantasy as Theodicy in George MacDonald's *Phantastes* and *Lilith*." *North Wind* 27 (2008) 16–34.

Seper, Charles. "C.S. Lewis." http://georgemacdonald.info/lewis.html

8

Red Tights and Red Tape

Satirical Misreadings of
The Screwtape Letters

David Mark Purdy

In this chapter, my purpose is to address the common assertion that C.S. Lewis's *The Screwtape Letters* is a satire, to demonstrate that this genre ascription constitutes a misreading that has been prevalent in the literary criticism of the novel since its initial publication, and to submit that "Screwtapean fantasy" is a more accurate and critically productive genre label. In the decades that have passed since *Screwtape* was first introduced to the world in 1941, critics have called the novel Lewis's "most popular work," a bestseller, and a masterpiece,[1] but the epithet that has attached itself most strongly to *Screwtape* is "satire." Although the passing years have not seen a decline in the novel's popularity, critical engagement with the work stagnated very early on. For this reason, uncritical repetition has replaced rational investigation in establishing the nature of the novel's genre. Very few critics who call *Screwtape* a satire make any effort to substantiate the claim, and no critics openly question it. The only published text that clearly identifies the need to approach this label with skepticism is not even a formal work of criticism; it is James Stobaugh's high school textbook *Skills for Literary Analysis*. Stobaugh expects that high

1. See Patrick, *Magdalen*,131; Benedict XVI, *Truth,* 184; Taliaferro & Traughber, "The Atonement," 252.

school students should find it obvious that the term "satire" is not applicable to *Screwtape*, and yet this possibility has never been acknowledged in the critical scholarship on the novel. This lack of ongoing critical dialogue has prevented scholars from realizing that *Screwtape* does not conform to the definition of satire as put forth by such literary authorities as M.H. Abrams.

According to Abrams, satire is "the literary art of diminishing or derogating a subject by making it ridiculous and evoking toward it attitudes of amusement, contempt, scorn, or indignation."[2] The three qualities essential to this definition are humor, derogation, and misrepresentation. If *Screwtape* is a satire, then, it must adhere comfortably within the definition of a satire by humorously derogating some subject by way of misrepresentation.

There are several possible objects of mockery in the novel because Screwtape (the character) falls into many categories that Lewis opposes. As a demon, he represents the work of the spiritual forces of evil. The demon caricature accompanying Lewis on the cover of the 8 September 1947 edition of *Time* magazine suggests that these are the forces that *Screwtape* satirizes.[3] Some critics have asserted that Screwtape is satirized as a red-tape-toting bureaucrat because, in his role as a prominent authority in the extremely bureaucratic Lowerarchy of Hell, Screwtape provides an allegorical parallel to human bureaucracies.[4] Thirdly, Screwtape is a representative of a particular set of worldviews that Lewis rejects because Screwtape propounds a variety of human ideologies. If the novel consistently mocked any of these positions through humorous misrepresentation, critics would be justified in labelling *Screwtape* a satire, but such is not the case. Demons and bureaucracies are characterized negatively in the novel, but these entities are presented with gravity and a profound recognition of their potential for wreaking havoc in the world. With very few exceptions, the subjects that the novel humorously criticizes are presented with sincerity and

2. Abrams and Harpham, *Glossary*, 284–85.

3. Christopher, *C.S. Lewis*, 78.

4. See Spivey, *Beyond Modernism*, 134; Leithart, "Screwtape Letters," 551; Painter, "Sympathy," 72–73.

not misrepresentation. As with the other objects of opposition, the opposition of human propensities and philosophies mostly fails to conform to Abrams's definition of satire: Screwtape's observations are sincere and do not mock any human teachings. Still, there are a few exceptions in which Screwtape derides ideas that some real people would knowingly defend. His discussions of constructing a historical Jesus and pursuing "Christianity And" both conform to all three of Abrams's criteria.

In addressing these rare exceptions, it is helpful to consider Lewis's distinction between satire and the satiric. This distinction, which has been recognized by many other scholars,[5] acknowledges "satire" as a genre while defining "the satiric" as an instantiation of that genre.[6] Because the examples of the satiric are so rare in *Screwtape*, they do not justify labelling the novel a satire. The satire-satiric distinction is a crucial one in genre studies as it is entirely misleading to call a novel a satire simply because it contains scattered instances of the satiric. The emphasis that scholarly accounts place on these rare occurrences of the satiric in *Screwtape* occludes other more integral literary techniques employed in the novel, such as narrative voice and moral inversion. There is much more misrepresentation *of* the novel than there is misrepresentation *in* the novel.

Moral inversion

One of the primary reasons that critics have unquestioningly accepted the claim that *Screwtape* is a satire is that the novel's extensive use of moral inversion has been compared with similar usages of moral inversion in the satirical works of Jonathan Swift, notably in *A Modest Proposal.*[7] Some critics who recognize this connection between the two writings appear to have labelled Lewis's novel a satire because Swift's essay is a satire. Of the two, only *A Modest*

---

5. See Abrams & Harpham, *Glossary*, 285.

6. Schakel, "Restoration," 193.

7. See Craig, *New Lamps*, 39; Filmer, *Scepticism*, 67; Knowles, "Screwtape Letters," 18.

Proposal consistently employs misrepresentation in its arguments. *Screwtape* does not become a satire by virtue of association with a satirical essay. The connection between the two writings is their prominent use of moral inversion; this inversion is the source of humor for both works. The claim that all writings that employ moral inversion are satires is a poor generalization. When identifying a genre that accurately describes *Screwtape*, therefore, the novel's moral inversion should be foregrounded.

Satire is not appropriate as a defining genre label for *Screwtape* because satire entails inaccurate representation. Most of the novel's themes are contingent upon the fact that both the narrator and the topics of his letters are sincere depictions of their real-world counterparts. Calling the novel a satire denies this. For this reason, a different label should be identified which acknowledges the novel's sincerity. While the connection critics have made with Swift's writings displays the centrality of moral inversion to the novel's genre, the primary literary device Lewis employs is double inversion. Single moral inversion is "a total reversal of values so that evil becomes good and good, evil."[8] Double inversion begins in the same manner, but it goes further. Novels that employ double inversion position the reader to morally invert a statement in the novel twice: the first inversion results from the reader's knowledge that Screwtape is evil, while the second results from the reader's perception that the first inversion unexpectedly produces a statement that appears evil. The ensuing explanation Screwtape provides for his seemingly uncharacteristic argument invites readers to question their previously held philosophies or reminds them of their foolish subconscious tendencies. The result is a rhetorical device that is both strong, because of the extra mental effort it requires, and humorous, because of the sudden incongruity it presents. Consequently, readers are able to undergo directed self-reflection in the context of non-threatening humorous incongruities.

The literary device of double inversion is implemented by Lewis at several key points in *Screwtape*. In Letter 28, for example, Screwtape harshly chastises Wormwood for his cheerfulness in

8. Holbrook, *Sex and Dehumanization*, 23.

reporting that his human patient is likely to be killed in an air raid. Screwtape goes on to explain that Wormwood's "chief aim at the moment should be the very same thing for which the patient's lover and his mother are praying – namely his bodily safety."[9] Because the nature of the novel thus far sets the reader up to invert the perspective of this statement, he or she will be faced with the suggestion that the death of Wormwood's human patient is a good thing. If Screwtape is against it, it must somehow contribute positively to the ultimate good of humankind. Screwtape quickly resolves the confusion by explaining that, if the patient dies in a state of grace, the state in which he currently abides, God will claim his soul for Heaven while the demons of Hell will never again be able to touch him. In this fashion, Lewis argues that the tendency of humans to "regard death as the prime evil and survival as the greatest good"[10] is simply demonic propaganda: that which is truly of lasting importance is spiritual death and spiritual life. As is revealed two letters later, both Wormwood's and Screwtape's predictions were correct: the man is killed in an air raid and his soul is expediently ushered into Heaven.[11] This literary device propels much of the novel. Screwtape makes a value judgement that appears to contradict his character; the inversion of the value judgement is insupportable when taken at face value; and Screwtape then divulges the reasoning behind his seemingly incongruous statement to reveal what the novel suggests is a subtle yet crucial flaw in society's established worldview.

The pattern of double inversion becomes evident from the very beginning of Screwtape's letters. In Letter 1, Screwtape tells Wormwood not to present arguments against Christianity into the mind of his patient, but the reader is not left wondering why arguments against Christianity would be detrimental to the cause of anti-Christian demons for long. Screwtape quickly elaborates that their goal should be to keep humans from approaching the Gospel on an intellectual level: humans should reject Christianity for

9. Lewis, *Screwtape*, 154.
10. Ibid., 154.
11. Ibid., 171–75.

aesthetic, emotional, or other similarly irrelevant reasons instead of considering it on logical grounds. Screwtape's justification for recommending this method of persuasion is that "reason and logic . . . both favor Christianity."[12] Lewis's reasoning behind ascribing such a tactic to demons is found in *Mere Christianity*, in which he poses the question, "[I]f you examined a hundred people who had lost their faith in Christianity, I wonder how many of them would turn out to have been reasoned out of it by honest argument? Do not most people simply drift away?"[13] Because Screwtape believes that honest pursuit of truth through logic will lead humans to become Christians, he advises Wormwood to avoid advancing reason-based arguments to his patient.

Similarly, in Letter 2, Screwtape makes the shocking declaration that "one of our greatest allies is the Church itself."[14] The reader soon discovers that what Screwtape means is that the shortcomings and external appearance of the members of the Church present demons with prime opportunities for causing humans to reject Christianity: the equation of "the church with the oddities of its individual members."[15] The suggestion is that Wormwood's patient must be persuaded to equate the inevitable failings of individual Christians with proof that Christianity is flawed.

In Letter 3, Screwtape suggests that Wormwood should encourage his patient to pray for his mother's spiritual well-being even though prayer for the spiritual health of others is a practice widely supported in Christian circles. Screwtape's explanation for this peculiar recommendation consists in the belief that a focus on his mother's spiritual well-being will distract the patient from concern about her practical needs, allowing the patient to simultaneously pray for his mother's soul and be inconsiderate to her in person without realizing the contradiction. As these examples from Screwtape's letters demonstrate, Lewis's double inversion is a

---

12. Schmidt, *How Christianity Changed the World*, 370.

13. Lewis, *Mere Christianity*, 141.

14. Lewis, *Screwtape*, 5.

15. Gibson, *C.S. Lewis*, 109.

prominent feature of the novel and should therefore be recognized in determining its genre.

The narrator's role

There are two aspects of *Screwtape*'s composition which are integral to the literary technique of double inversion and, hence, the novel's genre. These are its narrator and its moral dichotomy. The novel's narrator lends himself to double inversion because of the perspective he provides. This perspective is contingent on three aspects of his character:

1. his worldview inverts the one the novel implicitly supports;

2. he is sincerely dedicated to that worldview; and

3. he embodies an accurate representation of the worldview.

As Lewis himself put it, an author writing in this genre paints "the blacks all white and the whites all black."[16] In other words, the narrator diametrically inverts all valuations. The second of the novel's qualities integral to its use of double inversion is moral dichotomy. This element is key because it positions readers to morally invert everything Screwtape writes. In order for a novel to make use of double inversion, the novel must deal with a dichotomy whereby one of the two constituent perspectives necessarily alienates the reader and the other does not. The novel's narrator must embody the humanly insupportable worldview so that the reader is positioned to morally invert all of his or her statements. The narrator may then make statements that initially appear to be in the interests of the opposite perspective in order to create the double inversion. The dichotomy in *Screwtape* is the Biblical opposition of pure good and corrupted good as represented by God and demons, respectively. Because the narrator is a demon who desires the ultimate depravity of all humanity, his relationship with the reader is necessarily one of alienation; for this reason, the novel is able to make use of double inversion. Nonetheless, double

16. Cited in Lindvall, *Surprised by Laughter*, 262.

inversion is not restricted to Christian literature, as it is possible to apply other dichotomies to the technique.

Screwtapean fantasy, not satire

Unfortunately, no existing genre labels convey the primacy of double inversion. This technique works in *Screwtape* because the novel's premise depends on the immorality of all of the narrator's statements, thereby bringing moral inversion into play for every statement in the novel. Because narrators of novels in this genre must alienate all possible readers by embodying the opposite end of a moral dichotomy from that maintained by humans, the narrator must be a non-human entity. For this reason, the principal genre of *Screwtape* is a subgenre of fantasy. The validity of this genre ascription is strengthened by Brenton D.G. Dickieson's recent publication of the preface that Lewis originally wrote for *Screwtape*. The handwritten preface, held at Wheaton College's Marion E. Wade Center in Illinois, demonstrates that Lewis conceived of *Screwtape* as being a series of demonic letters that were intercepted and translated by Dr. Elwin Ransom, the protagonist of Lewis's *Space Trilogy*, a series of novels set, like *Screwtape*, during World War II.[17] The references to Ransom were removed from the preface for the publication of *Screwtape*, but the text was not altered in order to contradict Ransom's involvement. For this reason, it is consistent with the novel to consider the letters to have been translated by Ransom from Old Solar, the fictional language spoken by all beings in the Solar System in the *Space Trilogy* except humans.[18] The discovery of these few lost lines of the preface grounds *Screwtape* in the universe of the *Space Trilogy*. Consequently, it is reasonable to consider *Screwtape* a fantasy novel.

"Screwtapean fantasy" presents itself as an appropriate name for the specific genre of *Screwtape* because the genre's essential ideological reversal is encoded in Screwtape's name. The tape is

17. Dickieson, "Unpublished Preface," 296.

18. Ibid., 298.

a metaphor for Lewis's mediated textual communication to the reader and it is screwy because it has been inverted along the way. It is more helpful to call *Screwtape* a Screwtapean fantasy than a satire because this new label may be defined in such a way that it acknowledges the novel's use of unsatiric humor and highlights the double inversion. Furthermore, calling *Screwtape* a satire suggests that the novel's depiction of demons and the views they represent is not a sincere one. Indeed, the reality of evil is a theme of paramount importance in the novel, but the term "satire" diminishes this theme and dismisses the corresponding implications of Screwtape's arguments. Nonetheless, Screwtape's first letter demonstrates that what is crucial is not whether the label is "'academic' or 'practical', 'outworn' or 'contemporary', 'conventional' or 'ruthless'" but whether it is "'true' or 'false.'"[19] Since *Screwtape* does not correspond to the definition of satire, it does not matter whether calling the novel a satire is useful or agreeable: it is false. Future criticism must not continue to mischaracterize Screwtape as a satirical, caricatured, red-tape-toting demon in red tights. Acknowledging double inversion as the strength and ingenuity of *Screwtape* will establish Lewis's sincerity, in accordance with that of his narrator, and allow the rhetorical effectiveness of this literary technique to be recognized.

Bibliography

Abrams, M.H. and Geoffrey Galt Harpham. *A Glossary of Literary Terms,* 8th ed. Edited by Camille Adkins. Boston: Thomson Wadsworth, 2005.

Benedict XVI. *Truth and Tolerance: Christian Belief and World Religions.* Translated by Henry Taylor. San Francisco: Ignatius, 2004.

Christopher, Joe R. *C.S. Lewis.* Boston: Twayne, 1987.

Craig, Hardin. *New Lamps for Old: A Sequel to* The Enchanted Glass. Oxford: Blackwell, 1960.

Dickieson, Brenton D. G. "The Unpublished Preface to C.S. Lewis' *The Screwtape Letters.*" *Notes and Queries* 60, no. 2 (2013) 296–98.

Filmer, Kath. *Scepticism and Hope in Twentieth Century Fantasy Literature.* Bowling Green, OH: Bowling Green University Popular Press, 1992.

19. Lewis, *Screwtape,* 1.

Gibson, Evan K. *C.S. Lewis: Spinner of Tales: A Guide to His Fiction*. Washington, DC: Christian University Press, 1980.

Holbrook, David. *Sex and Dehumanization*. New Brunswick, NJ: Transaction, 1998.

Knowles, Jack L. "*The Screwtape Letters*: Of Greed and Grace." In *Beyond Aslan: Essays on C.S. Lewis*, edited by Burton K. Janes, 17–28. Gainesville, FL: Bridge-Logos, 2006.

Leithart, O. Woelke. "The Screwtape Letters." In *Omnibus I: Biblical and Classical Civilizations*, edited by Douglas Wilson and G. Tyler Fischer, 551–62. Lancaster, PA: Veritas, 2005.

Lewis, C.S. *Mere Christianity*. San Francisco: HarperCollins, 2001.

———. *The Screwtape Letters*. San Francisco: HarperCollins, 2001.

Lindvall, Terry. *Surprised by Laughter: The Comic World of C. S. Lewis*. Nashville, TN: Thomas Nelson, 1996.

Painter, Rebecca M. "*Sympathy for the Devil?*: A Historical Tour of Literature and Cultural Representation." In *The Enigma of Good and Evil: The Moral Sentiment in Literature*, edited by Anna-Teresa Tymieniecka, 65–76. Dordrecht: Springer, 2005.

Patrick, James. *The Magdalen Metaphysicals: Idealism and Orthodoxy at Oxford, 1901–1945*. Macon, GA: Mercer University Press, 1985.

Schakel, Peter J. "Restoration and Eighteenth Century." In *Reading the Classics with C.S. Lewis*, edited by Thomas L. Martin, 187–202. Grand Rapids, MI: Baker Academic, 2000.

Schmidt, Alvin J. *How Christianity Changed the World*. Grand Rapids, MI: Zondervan, 2004.

Spivey, Ted R. *Beyond Modernism: Toward a New Myth Criticism*. Lanham, MD: University Press of America, 1988.

Stobaugh, James P. *Skills for Literary Analysis: Teacher Edition*. Nashville, TN: B&H, 2005.

Swift, Jonathan. *A Modest Proposal and Other Satirical Works*. Edited by Stanley Appelbaum. Mineola, NY: Dover Thrift, 1996.

Taliaferro, Charles and Rachel Traughber. "The Atonement in Narnia." In *The Chronicles of Narnia and Philosophy: The Lion, the Witch, and the Worldview*, edited by Gregory Bassham and Jerry L. Walls, 245–59. Peru, IL: Carus, 2005.

9

The Eschatology and "Amen" of C.S. Lewis

Sarah Layman

E schatology, once considered among the seven main branches of theological studies along with Christology and ecclesiology, has today become a watchword for identifying quacks and doom-sayers who profess the ability to predict the exact time of the "end of days." The doctrine of the eschaton – the End – has fallen from its original prominence in theological discussion to spurring on the creation of popular movies such as *Armageddon* and *2012*. Belief in the reality of the eschaton is not a pressing issue in the daily lives of most Christians today. Ministers avoid talking about it for fear of creating panic, theologians avoid talking about it because the New Testament writers' sense of urgency about the second coming has been lost, and everyday Christians avoid thinking about it because they do not understand, as C.S. Lewis demonstrates, that the end is really the beginning. The "further up and further in" we go into the coming Kingdom, the better things will be.

Yet, as Christians, when we profess our faith through the Nicene Creed, we claim to believe in Jesus' return to judge the living and the dead, in the resurrection of the dead, and in the life to come after death. If we claim to believe it, why do we not live as though we do? There is a strange disconnect between many Christians' professed faith in the eschaton and their lack of theological praxis about its reality. Talk of the eschaton has not been removed entirely from Christian discourse, however: it still takes its place in regular lectionary readings and appears in the creeds. Even so, as Chad Walsh points out, the "Amen" at the end of the Nicene Creed, which affirms our belief in all that we have just professed, is said with the casual assumption that the catastrophic end of history has not occurred in the last few million years and is not likely to occur soon.[1] Our response to the creeds puts us in a position similar to that of St. Augustine prior to his conversion. Augustine used to pray for God to work on his heart and take him away from his wicked ways—but not yet.[2] In our "Amen" at the end of the creed, we cling to Augustine's "not yet." We profess to look eagerly towards the resurrection of the dead and the life to come, but follow it with a whisper of "not yet." Many are afraid of what will come next, and what the consequences will be of letting go of our present world and all that it contains. We are reluctant to let go of our worldly pleasures, even for the promise of heavenly splendor.

For some Christians, however, there is a pressing need to release that "not yet," and to fully embrace the "Amen" at the end of the creed as we are called to do. C.S. Lewis was one of these Christians. Lewis viewed the eschaton as something to be anticipated and eagerly hoped for, because it would bring about the creation of a new heaven and a new earth. This hope is evident in many of his writings, especially *The Last Battle*. When Lewis uttered the word "Amen" at the end of the Nicene Creed, it seems clear that he did so with the conviction that the eschaton will arrive, and with it, the consummation of the whole world. Lewis's eschatological understandings offer a challenge to take that "Amen" seriously, and to await with eagerness the Second Coming of Christ and the perfection of all creation. This paper will explore Lewis's treatment of eschatology by focusing specifically on *The Last Battle,* which provides us with significant insight into his approach to the doctrine.

---

1. Walsh, "Last Things," 25.

2. See Augustine's *Confessions* for his struggle regarding conversion and his reluctance to let go of his former ways.

"The End" in Lewis's fiction

The themes of the eschaton and the finality of this world resonate within several of Lewis's works of fiction. Lewis had a particular way of writing fiction that conveyed theological themes without naming within the narrative the specifically Christian content. Lewis never wrote a theological treatise on the eschaton,[3] and was not trying to paint a picture of the physical reality of the End in his fiction. He introduced theological materials obliquely, rather than directly, offering his readers the opportunity to use their imaginations in new ways. He encouraged them to consider his narrative worlds and their respective ends in his stories, thereby providing the link to questioning our world and our place within it.

The doctrine of the eschaton is a pivotal part of Christian theology since it proclaims the return of Christ to complete the Kingdom of God. Testimony about the end of days is offered in the Nicene and Apostles' creeds as well as in lectionary readings. The affirmations that Christ will return and that our earthly world will pass away are professed in Christian congregations around the world every Sunday. We have, perhaps, lost the sense of urgency about this, as we find it among the writers of the New Testament. Lewis looked to Jesus' resurrection as that which made possible the start of the new creation. In *Miracles*, he writes:

> The New Testament writers speak as if Christ's achievement in rising from the dead was the first event of its kind in the whole history of the universe. He is the "first fruits," the "pioneer of life." He has forced open a door that has been locked since the death of the first man. He has met, fought and beaten the King of Death. Everything is different because He has done so. This is the beginning of the New Creation: a new chapter in cosmic history has opened.[4]

---

3. See Lewis, *World's Last Night*, for a related treatment.

4. Lewis, *Miracles*, 173.

It is clear that, for Lewis, nothing after the resurrection can be the same. There is a fundamental difference in the world after Golgotha, which marks the beginning of the end to come.

As noted above, through the Nicene Creed the faithful profess to look for the resurrection of the dead and the life of the world to come. In the first two weeks of Advent, the lectionary readings similarly speak of waiting for and anticipating Christ's return and of the coming of the Kingdom of God. What for most Christians is a remote eventuality, however, becomes in Lewis's books "a poetically vivid certainty."[5] For Lewis, as for the apostle Paul, Christ is the new Adam through whom humanity is to be restored to its original harmony with God. This final restoration will mean that humanity will once again have the same command over nature that Lewis attributes to the first humans.[6] The coming of Christ is only the beginning of the new creation and the end of this world. Lewis uses this sense of longing for the true Kingdom throughout his works, especially in *The Last Battle*.

The Last Battle is the final book in the *Chronicles of Narnia* series. Although these fantasy books are not allegorical stories, they contain many Christian themes and images that explore theological concepts such as the eschaton. If *The Magician's Nephew* responds to the desire to know of the beginning of things, *The Last Battle* addresses the need for knowledge about the end.[7] In *The Last Battle*, "Lewis pictures for us the eschatological end of everything, when the world of Narnia has been made new and the old things have passed away."[8] The novel presents its readers with one account of the end of creation and of the world after it has been made anew. Throughout the narrative, Lewis invites his readers to join in and contemplate the meaning and reality of the end of evil and the formation of a new creation that consists of all that is good. The end of Narnia and the subsequent creation of the new

5. Walsh, "Last Things," 26.

6. Ibid., 29.

7. Schakel, *Reading With The Heart*, 115.

8. Provan, "In The Stable," 161.

Narnia mark the end of an adventure. The end of one story is only the beginning of another story, a story that has no end.

Throughout the book, the reader can sense something is not quite right in Narnia: despite the appearance of small victories as the story progresses, it is clear that something dreadful will happen by the end. The book begins with the words, "In the last days of Narnia[.]"[9] When King Tirian is introduced, he is called "the last of the Kings of Narnia."[10] The end of Narnia seems inevitable, and even the most oblivious reader cannot help but perceive the unfolding drama of apocalypse and redemption.[11] The Pevensie children in the *Narnia* stories previously discovered Narnia to be a wonderful place—a magical land of talking animals and trees. The thought of Narnia ending is troubling for them because they do not understand that the impending end is just the beginning. The children do not understand that Narnia has been contaminated with evil, and that the only way to purify it to its original state is to destroy and make it anew. The children are afraid of what will happen to Narnia, and they are especially afraid of losing Aslan.

The old Narnia has to be destroyed, however. As the story comes to its climax, all the good of the old Narnia is drawn into the new through the stable door, as Aslan separates the animals to his left and to his right. When all of the Narnian creatures are forced to appear before their Lion, one of two reactions is possible: either the creature recognizes its Lion and is filled with utter love, passing to his right and beyond him to the new Narnia; or else it sees only a terrible beast and swerves to his left into the eternal darkness that is apart from him.[12] This scene from *The Last Battle* brings to mind the parable of the sheep and goats from Matthew 25:31–46. Lewis insisted over and over that his stories are not meant to be allegorical, and this scene is no exception. The animals' turning to left or right has nothing to do with pre-destination; it is instead about recognition and relationship. Lewis uses this event to illus-

---

9. Lewis, *Last Battle*, 1.

10. Ibid., 15.

11. Bell, "Inside the Wardrobe," 13.

12. Connolly, *Inklings*, 16.

trate the necessity of having a relationship with Aslan, the creator of Narnia, in order to be admitted into the new creation. Knowing Aslan constitutes a relationship of pure love. Lewis here encourages his readers to consider the relationship they have with their own "Lion," the triune God.

Narnian apocalypse

Lewis's vivid imagery indicates that the end of Narnia is terrible and real. The creatures are called to meet Aslan face to face; the stars are drawn out of the sky leaving everything pitch black; the land floods with water; and the sun and moon are destroyed by Father Time. Here Lewis advances a theory, via the narrative, about how the end of the world might occur. He takes this a step further and envisions what the new world might be like: "The air of the new Narnia is no longer 'thick' with the effects of evil. Now it is pure, clean, exhilarating air that does not impede any action or thought."[13] Upon entering the new Narnia, the children realize that this is actually the real Narnia, and that the old Narnia was only a shadow. The new Narnia is much bigger, the colors are much more vivid, and the limitations that existed in the old Narnia no longer apply. All of the characters that they meet in the new Narnia continually urge them to go "further up and further in" because the inside of the new Narnia is bigger than the outside. Digory and Polly look much younger than they did in the other world; Edmund's knees no longer hurt; the children can run all day without getting tired; and they can all keep up with the fastest animals without losing their breath. The new Narnia is a magical place where all limitations have vanished, and there is no taint of evil.

The end of the old Narnia is not really an ending at all, but the start of a new beginning that will last forever. This has implications for how Lewis understood the end of our own world: his "inclusion of England as part of the new lands shows that he means this

13. Williams, *Heart of the Chronicles*, 166.

picture to be more than mere fantasy. Not only is the Narnia of his imagination to be restored, but also all that is good of the real earth."[14] The inclusion of England in the new Narnia is meant to signal that this is a renewal of the whole created order. Readers are meant to come to know that this wonderful regeneration and renewal is meant for our world too, not only the fantasy land of Narnia.

When examining Lewis's eschatology, it is critical to remember that for Lewis the End is always a new beginning. The new is not a carbon copy of the old, because the new is fundamentally different—it is free of evil and all physical limitations. In *The Last Battle*, all that was good in the old Narnia is contained within the new Narnia. Lewis reinforces this difference between a repetition of the old world and the creation of a new one by portraying the End of Narnia taking place in reverse order, relative to the first creation story in Genesis. In Genesis, the earth begins as a dark formless void, then dark and light are separated with the creation of day and night. The waters are separated to make dry land. God creates the living creatures, and finally humankind.[15] This account begins at the stage in which, in contrast, Narnia comes to an end. When Aslan stands at the door of the new Narnia, the world around him ends in a sequence that reverses the Genesis events: the humans and talking animals pass by Aslan first; then beasts in the form of dragons and giant lizards roam the earth; the waters stretch out to create a watery void; light and dark collide; the sun and moon become one; and finally complete darkness takes over and the old Narnia is no more. Lewis uses this imagery to prompt readers' theological imaginations to wrestle with the idea that the new Narnia is a new Creation that will bring about the fullness of life and the consummation of all things in our world also.

14. Ibid., 168.
15. Gen 1:1–27.

The perfection of creation

Another vital aspect of Lewis's eschatology is the idea of perfection.[16] For Lewis, the concept of perfection takes its place not only in his eschatological understanding of humankind, but also in the perfection of creation as a whole. His depiction of the destruction of Narnia brings the existence of the world full circle, finishing where it began. The destruction of the world at the eschaton matches its creation in circular perfection. Lewis is not trying to imagine directly how God will undertake the End, but rather is trying to work through a theology of the eschaton that takes into account the principles of the creeds. As Sean Connolly points out:

> In his work, the rich imagery with which C.S. Lewis presented his eschatological worldview was anything but an attempt to say what the End of Time might actually be like. Rather he furnished us with a cataphatic springboard from which to enter into the apophatic mystery at the heart of God himself.[17]

The Last Battle creates a sense of longing in the reader for the new Narnia, which the descriptions of it cannot satisfy. Instead "the sense of longing is increased by the descriptions of the new Narnia, by the reappearance of characters from the previous books, and by the knowledge that although this is the last of the books, it is not the end of the real story."[18] Lewis wanted to imply some sense of the "real" story of the life and world to come, and how that real story might start only after the End. When Aslan tells the children, "The dream is ended: this is the morning,"[19] the suggestion is that the children have died and are now in Heaven, their true home. For the first time, they are now fully alive.[20] They are no longer subject to the limitations of this world, and instead are free

---

16. Connolly, *Inklings*, 18.
17. Ibid., 278.
18. Schakel, *The Way Into Narnia*, 113.
19. Lewis, *Last Battle*, 228.
20. Williams, *Heart of the Chronicles*, 165.

from the "thick air" and heaviness that surrounds us. They are free from evil and the shadows present in the old Narnia.

Lewis's eschatology is not entirely straightforward: "It involves 'the end of the world,' but that end is the real beginning. It will bring about a transformed nature, heal schisms, and mark the culmination of the constantly increasing distinctness of good and evil."[21] While Lewis never composed a theological treatise on eschatology as such, it is clear that his eschatological imagination was operative in his fictional works. Indeed, it seems clear that for Lewis the "Amen" at the end of the Nicene Creed would have been more than a casual affirmation of the resurrection of the dead and the world to come. Lewis believed that the eschaton was a reality waiting to occur and something that we can eagerly anticipate. As he writes in *The World's Last Night*,

> We can, perhaps, train ourselves to ask more and more often how the thing which we are saying or doing (or failing to do) at each moment will look when the irresistible light streams upon it; that light which is so different from the light of this world—and yet, even now, we know just enough of it to take it into account.[22]

Lewis did not believe that we should stand around waiting for the End, or attempt to keep ourselves in a constant state of anticipation for its arrival. Instead, he suggested that the important thing was always to remember and take it into account. For Lewis, it is essential to expect that the Second Coming will happen, to admit that we cannot possibly find out when, and to keep ourselves ready for it.[23] These are necessary if the "Amen" at the end of the creed is to be taken seriously.

While Lewis did not intend to provide an exact account of how the End will occur, his works that relate to eschatology are meant to encourage his readers to remember the resurrection and to take note of what they profess when they pray for the Kingdom

21. Walsh, "Last Things," 29.
22. Lewis, *World's Last Night*, 110.
23. Ibid., 113.

to come. Lewis's own "Amen" contains an active attempt to understand the eschaton and what it means for the living of our days. It is my hope that texts like the *The Last Battle* and *The World's Last Night* will encourage in readers for generations to come that same desire to acknowledge the importance of the eschaton. May our "Amen" at the end of the creed be more than a casual affirmation and instead become a joyful anticipation of the resurrection of the dead and the hope of the world to come.

Bibliography

Bell, Robert H. "Inside the Wardrobe: Is 'Narnia' a Christian Allegory?" *Commonweal* 135, no. 22 (16 Dec 2005) 12–17.

Connolly, Sean. *Inklings of Heaven: C.S. Lewis and Eschatology*. Herefordshire: Gracewing, 2007.

Lewis, C.S. *The Last Battle*. New York: HarperCollins, 1984.

———. *Miracles*. New York: HarperCollins, 1996.

———. *The World's Last Night and Other Essays*. New York: Harcourt, 1960.

Provan, Iain W. "In The Stable With Dwarves: Testimony, Interpretation, Faith, and the History of Israel." In *Windows into Old Testament History: Evidence, Argument, and the Crisis of 'Biblical Israel'*, edited by V. Philips Long, David W. Baker, and Gordon J. Wenham, 161–97. Grand Rapids, MI: Eerdmans, 2002.

Schakel, Peter. *Reading With The Heart: The Way Into Narnia*. Grand Rapids, MI: Eerdmans, 1979.

———. *The Way Into Narnia: A Reader's Guide*. Grand Rapids, MI: 2005

Walsh, Chad. "Last Things First Things: The Eschatology of C.S. Lewis." *Theology Today* 6 (1949) 25–30.

Williams, Thomas. *The Heart of the Chronicles of Narnia*. Nashville, TN: Thomas Nelson, 2005.

10

The Space Between

Observations From the Threshold

———————— *Wayne G. Smith* ————————

The Pevensie children spend the most time, and their most in-tense time, in *The Lion, the Witch and the Wardrobe* involved with the first two characters of the book's title.[1] The wardrobe, although inanimate, provides the initial animation of the young travellers into Narnia; it is a vehicle into further understanding of their journey and a caution for our own. It is such an *aide memoire* to the secret world of Narnia that the wardrobe is memorialized in bronze in the city of the author's birth.[2] In haste towards the mys-teries of Narnia itself, I may have, in the past, stepped too quickly over the threshold of this third fundamental "character." My pur-pose here is to linger in the wardrobe, to see if there are further mysteries hidden within its bounds, and to explore its function as a mediator of a relational ontology and its allusions to a theology of being.

I cautiously suggest here that the wardrobe occupies the nar-rative's most significant threshold, even though the Lion, Aslan, is never more analogous to the Jesus of Lewis's Christian tradition

1. Lewis, *The Lion.*

2. A life-sized bronze statue of Lewis, poised to enter a wardrobe, stands outside Holywood Arches at the Holywood Road library in East Belfast. This work, "The Searcher," by sculptor Ross Wilson, was unveiled in 1998, the cen-tenary of Lewis's birth.

than in his sacrificial offering upon the Stone Table, a location that points to the threshold between life and death. Observations about the Table are addressed here first in order to contrast it with what I suggest is, for the story's human protagonists, the more ontologically efficacious threshold of the wardrobe. Although the return of Aslan from the dead is certainly of ultimate significance for the restoration of Narnia's normal seasons (and not merely deliverance from the grip of eternal winter), Aslan is not essentially changed by his time on the Table. This contrasts with the transformations experienced by the children by means of their wardrobe/threshold.

Christians may be drawn to extend the analogy of Aslan's time on the Stone Table to discussions of Christ's whereabouts between Good Friday and Easter Sunday. By way of the Table, the messianic lion enters a threshold state analogous to the Pevensies in their wardrobe/threshold experience. This state of being is appropriately captured in T.S. Eliot's "Burnt Norton."[3] Lewis's Christian view of the transitional "still point" necessarily turns the threshold of the Stone Table into the site of a state of being for the Lion, the true nature of which is unknown by the citizens of Narnia and (temporarily) grieved by their unknowing would-be Kings and Queens. Lewis believed that the time and space between life and death comprised a purifying cleansing. In private correspondence, he equated the threshold of death and (resurrected) life with the concept of purgatory. One of his interpretations of the Western Church's doctrine of purgatory was that of a cleansing dental rinse, which would necessarily follow death as a type of tooth extraction.[4] Alternatively, he also opined that the soul's time in purgatory is awash in a type of chaos through which men learn to take responsibility and women learn to give up feeling overly responsible.[5]

In contrast, the threshold of the wardrobe is not purgatorial for the child protagonists, although it is transitional. The children become something they were not previously, even though their

3. This poem may be viewed online on a variety of websites.

4. Lewis, *Yours*, 323.

5. Ibid., 359.

self-perception takes time to be changed as they grow into the roles expected of them in Narnia. Threshold space—and whatever existential-spiritual time and activity of transition that a person (real or imagined) spends in one—has been described as "the limit, the boundary, the frontier that distinguishes and opposes two worlds—and at the same time the paradoxical place where those two worlds communicate, where passage from the profane to the sacred world becomes possible." As a result, thresholds are "symbols and at the same time vehicles of passage from the one space to the other."[6] Encounters on thresholds are necessarily transitional: they can feel like a place that is neither "here" nor "there," neither "then" nor "now," and yet are both. Travellers are, for a time, in both times and spaces, yet in neither one wholly. A.A. Milne's poem "Halfway Down" is instructive.[7] The wardrobe, like a point partway up/down a staircase, is "somewhere else" indeed. As perceived from within the wardrobe, the two external worlds both bookend the threshold and constitute/reconstitute its contents. In its passageway, coats transition into trees, mothballs transform into snow, and the children begin moving toward their new birth as Narnian royalty.[8]

Toward a new birth

The use of "new birth," and its implication of the requirement of some assistance, is not accidental here. Alister McGrath describes Lewis as a literary "midwife."[9] Might the children's own curiosity fulfill the role of a rebirth midwife, encouraging their emergence into Narnia? The image of the wardrobe as the birth canal of the children's maturity into kings and queens of Narnia presents an unavoidable analogy to the liminal process of actual birth. Questions and mystery surround the about-to-be-born as well as the

6. Eliade, *Sacred*, 25.

7. This poem may be viewed online on a variety of websites.

8. Lewis, *The Lion*, 7.

9. This refers to Lewis's influence on J.R.R. Tolkien's *Lord of the Rings*. See McGrath's preface to McGrath, *C.S. Lewis*.

vessels of their delivery during the birthing process. So too for the human co-workers of the Christ figure in Narnia: the Sons of Adam and the Daughters of Eve hail from the mysterious "far land of Spare Oom where eternal summer reigns around the bright city of War Drobe."[10] Yet Lewis, although he was biologically childless, observed elsewhere that the transitions of maternity are a time of hard work, analogous to the hard and long winter of Narnia's environment-in-exile from new life during which "[p]erpetual springtime is not allowed."[11] Sons and Daughters of Adam and Eve know that the world from which they came is not all summer or springtime, but this reality is set aside as new responsibilities fall on them in Narnia, on the other side of the threshold. Nor can one enter the same transitional state a second time: "You won't get into Narnia again by *that* route,"[12] advises the children's host on the England side of the wardrobe.[13]

The journey across/through a life-changing threshold is the beginning of the end of one world and the end of the beginning of its counterpart on the other side. The overlap boundary/threshold of the highly metaphorical wardrobe appears able to narrow or widen, depending upon the developmental need of that which is passing through it *en route* to its new destination. Consider that, at one point, Peter wonders about the existential width and depth of the threshold he is experiencing: "I suppose this whole country is in the wardrobe."[14]

Ethnographer Arnold van Gennep observed three stages in crossing a threshold: separation, transition, and incorporation.[15] The liminal (from the Latin *limen*, "threshold") is that second stage "characterized by being passed through; i.e. the purpose of this period is to transfer the subject from the original site to the

10. Lewis, *The Lion*, 13.

11. Lewis, *Yours*, 268.

12. Lewis, *The Lion*, 205; emph. added.

13. Cf. John 3:4: "How can anyone be born after having grown old? Can one enter a second time into the mother's womb and be born?"

14. Lewis, *The Lion*, 61.

15. van Gennep, *Rites of Passage*, 11.

new site."[16] The secret door of the wardrobe provides the liminality needed for that transference to occur. The discipline of modern midwifery can pose existential questions from the wisdom of its mysteries: "If there were a secret door to birth, to giving birth, what would it look like? What's behind, around, or in front of it? Is anyone in the picture?"[17] As a partial answer, the children are drawn into and through the threshold, seeking "an enlargement of [their] being."[18] As rewarding and exciting as the liminal transition may be, it is still scary and not wholly within the control of those directly involved. The birthing analogy continues: on a number of occasions, Lewis-as-narrator intervenes in the story to express, on behalf of the children, their fearful thoughts of being trapped or experiencing a breeching in the process.[19] Thresholds are meant to be passed over, not rested upon or rested within.

Just as the physical first-birthing process is one of "intimacy and privacy,"[20] so it is with the existential-spiritual rebirth through liminal space. Lewis tells of the secretive nature of the children's discoveries and their concern as to whether or not the professor (their host and guardian) would believe their account. He notes the professor's caution about sharing their experiences with anyone "unless they've had adventures of the same sort themselves."[21]

New knowledge, new being

A special knowledge has been acquired by the young pilgrims in their final transition back over the threshold. The cells in their bodies may have forgotten what they've learned in their Narnian maturation but there has been renewal of each mind[22] followed

---

16. Wright, "Liminal."

17. England and Horowitz, *Birthing*, 38.

18. Edwards, "C.S. Lewis."

19. These sentiments are voiced respectively on behalf of characters Lucy, Peter, and Edmund; the latter defies this caution. Lewis, *The Lion*, 6, 7, 29, 57.

20. Gaskin, *Ina May Gaskin's Guide*, 170.

21. Lewis, *The Lion*, 206.

22. Cf. Rom 12:2.

inevitably by a new *gnosis* that cannot be forced or grasped, just as the metaphorical entrance/exit "cannot be opened at will and [does] not respond to commands."[23] In this space and its new knowing, relationships are persuasive, not coercive; and they refer outside of themselves, bearing significance beyond the wisdom of the interface moment.

There are even aspects of quantum theory expressed in our relational ontology as individuals and as members of societies. Our behavior—as did that of the Pevensies—reflects that of photons: first, we are often determined by what is contextually required at the time;[24] second, we are sometimes individual particles, each with our own soul-travels reflecting our respective hidden person-alities, as were Edmund, Lucy, Peter, and Susan; and, third, some-times we behave as quantum waves, part of and representative of a larger movement. The latter is seen in elements throughout *The Lion, The Witch, and the Wardrobe,* such as the children's identity being initially more comprehensible to Narnians as part of the nameless collective known as the Sons of Adam and the Daughters of Eve. The wardrobe birthed that change and its threshold stands poised for their returning re-transformation.

The potential for the transformation of life in both England and Narnia perhaps reveals Lewis's hopes for the reconciliation of "our" world, given the story's setting within the Second World War. Life on both sides of Lewis's wardrobe was awash in relation-ships broken by war, a reality that Victor Frankl knew well. From his Holocaust experience, Frankl derived an ontology of meaning based on his observation that everyone needs three things to be and to stay truly alive: something to do; someone to meet or some-thing to experience; and some way to address and to process occa-sions of suffering.[25] All three existential motivators were in play for the Pevensies, and for us with them, as they crossed the threshold of the wardrobe into Narnia. With them, we discover the overlap

23. Gaskin, *Ina May Gaskin's Guide,* 170.

24. "Whether we see a photon behaving as a wave or a particle depends on the sort of experiment we conduct." Al-Khalili, *Quantum,* 110.

25. Frankl, *Man's Search,* 133.

of existential-spiritual relations with their inherent beginnings, endings, and spaces between. Paradoxically, the new beginning signified by each new threshold also means, as Lewis himself observes, "the very end of the adventure of the wardrobe."[26]

Let us not step through too quickly.

Bibliography

Al-Khalili, Jim. *Quantum: A Guide for the Perplexed*. London: Weidenfield & Nicolson, 2003.

Edwards, Bruce D. "C.S. Lewis and the case for responsible scholarship." Discovery Institute, 1998. http://www.discovery.org/a/517.

Eliade, Mircea. *The Sacred and the Profane: The Nature of Religion*. Translated by Willard R. Trask. New York: Harcourt, Brace and Company, 1959.

England, Pam and Rob Horowitz. *Birthing from Within: An Extra-Ordinary Guide to Childbirth Preparation*. Albuquerque, NM: Partera, 1998.

Frankl, Viktor E. *Man's Search for Meaning*. New York: Washington Square, 1959.

Gaskin, Ina May. *Ina May Gaskin's Guide to Childbirth*. New York: Bantam, 2003.

Lewis, C.S. *The Lion, the Witch, and the Wardrobe*. New York: Harper Collins, 1950.

———. *Yours*. Edited by Paul F. Ford. New York: HarperCollins, 1950.

McGrath, Alister. *C.S. Lewis—A Life: Eccentric Genius, Reluctant Prophet*. N.P.: Tyndale House, 2013.

Van Gennep, Arnold. *The Rites of Passage*. Translated by Monika B. Vizedom and Gabrielle L. Caffee. Chicago: University of Chicago Press, 1960.

Wright, Allison. "Liminal." The Chicago School of Media Theory. http://lucian. uchicago.edu/blogs/mediatheory/keywords/liminal/.

26. Lewis, *The Lion*, 206.